Cambodia

Andrew Spooner

D0921652

Credits

Footprint credits

Editor: Jo Williams
Production and layout: Emma Bryers
Maps: Kevin Feeney

Managing Director: Andy Riddle
Commercial Director: Patrick Dawson
Publisher: Alan Murphy
Publishing Managers: Felicity Laughton,
Jo Williams, Nicola Gibbs
Marketing and Partnerships Director:
Liz Harper
Marketing Executive: Liz Eyles
Trade Product Manager: Diane McEntee
Account Managers: Paul Bew, Tania Ross
Advertising: Renu Sibal, Elizabeth Taylor
Trade Product Co-ordinator: Kirsty Holmes

Photography credits

Front cover: Angkor Wat, Taolmor/
Dreamstime
Back cover: Royal Palace, Phnom Penh,
Xuanlu Wang/Shutterstock

Printed and bound in the United States
of America

Every effort has been made to ensure that
the facts in this guidebook are accurate.
However, travellers should still obtain advice
from consulates, airlines, etc, about travel
and visa requirements before travelling.
The authors and publishers cannot accept
responsibility for any loss, injury or
inconvenience however caused.

Publishing information

Footprint *Focus Cambodia*
1st edition
© Footprint Handbooks Ltd
October 2012

ISBN: 978 1 908206 87 9
CIP DATA: A catalogue record for this book
is available from the British Library

® Footprint Handbooks and the Footprint
mark are a registered trademark of
Footprint Handbooks Ltd

Published by Footprint
6 Riverside Court
Lower Bristol Road
Bath BA2 3DZ, UK
T +44 (0)1225 469141
F +44 (0)1225 469461
footprinttravelguides.com

Distributed in the USA by Globe Pequot
Press, Guilford, Connecticut

The content of Footprint *Focus Cambodia*
has been taken directly from Footprint's
Southeast Asia Handbook which was
researched and written by Andrew Spooner
and Paul Dixon.

Contents

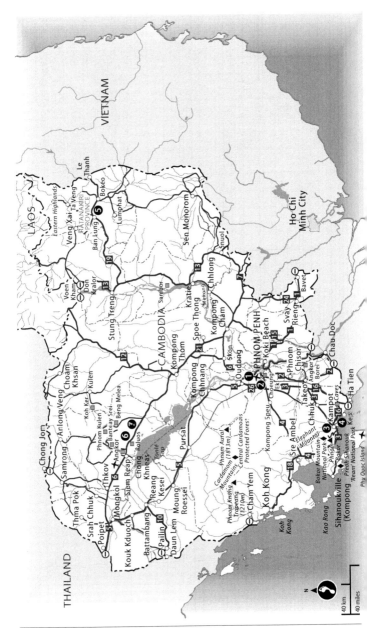

Impenetrable jungles; abandoned temples smothered in centuries of foliage; arcing white-sand beaches fringed with swaying palms; exotic, smiling locals – in almost every respect Cambodia satisfies the hackneyed expectations of Southeast Asia. And, if you get off the beaten track, Cambodia also offers that increasingly elusive feeling of discovery; the feeling that you are entering into arcane and unknown worlds where few Westerners have been before. But this is a country that is still trying to make sense of itself after the horrors of the genocidal Khmer Rouge rule. While the UN-sponsored trial of the former leaders finally got underway in 2007, many of its minor officials still hold positions of influence and power in Cambodia and you don't have to spend long in the country to see the gulf between the indifferent rich and the absolute poor.

Yet, without doubt, ancient Cambodia produced one of the world's greatest civilizations at Angkor. This temple complex near Siem Reap is truly breathtaking. But don't just stop there; Angkor Wat is merely one temple at the heart of a thousand others.

Today's capital, Phnom Penh, with its charming riverside setting is rapidly shedding its laid-back dusty charm and becoming a dynamic city complete with Hummer-driving Khmer yuppies, chic bars serving cocktails, clubs with designer interiors and hangouts filled with the great and the gorgeous.

On the beaches to the south you can find relaxed resort towns on the coast, such as Kep. In the northeastern provinces, tracts of red earth cut through hills carpeted in jungle. At Ban Lung you won't be disappointed by the waterfalls, boat rides and the stunning, bottle-green waters of Yaek Lom Lake.

Planning your trip

Getting to Cambodia

Air

Most travellers will need to route themselves through Bangkok, as it is generally the cheapest regional hub and offers the best connections with Phnom Penh and Siem Reap.

Boat

There are sailings from Ho Chi Minh City (Saigon) to Phnom Penh. Saigon tour cafés run minibuses to Chau Doc and on to the border, which is crossed on foot. Change to a speed boat which will take you to Neak Luong in Cambodia. Disembark here and take a taxi/pickup along Route 1 to Phnom Penh. From Stung Treng to the Laos border either charter a speed boat, which will take approximately 1½ hours, or board the slow ferry that leaves daily at around 0730 and takes approximately 3½ hours.

Road

It is possible to enter Cambodia, overland, from Thailand, Vietnam and Laos. Travellers coming from Thailand usually cross at Poipet where they'll find a recently completed fast road to Siem Reap. There are now overland entries from Thailand through Pailin (very rough roads) and Koh Kong, where new roads have also been completed (the boat from Koh Kong to Sihanoukville no longer operates). The overland route from Vietnam via Moc Bai is the slow but cheap option for travellers coming from the east, and the border crossing at Omsano has enabled those coming from Vietnam to take the more scenic river route via Chau Doc. There is a new scenic border open via Kep between Cambodia and Vietnam (Ha Tien). There is also a crossing between Phnom Penh and Tinh Bien in Vietnam. The border crossing with Laos, close to the town at Stung Treng.

Transport in Cambodia

Air

At the moment the only domestic route within Cambodia that operates safely and with any frequency is between Phnom Penh and Siem Reap. National carrier, **Cambodia Angkor Air**, flies this route but its website, www.cambodiaangkorair.com, doesn't allow bookings; their office in Phnom Penh is at 1-2/294 Mao Tse Tung, T023-666 6786. All departure taxes are now included in your fare.

Boat

All the Mekong towns and settlements around the Tonlé Sap are accessible by boat. It is a very quick and relatively comfortable way of travel and much cheaper than flying. The route between Siem Reap and Phnom Penh is very popular, while the route between Siem Reap and Battambang is one of the most scenic. With the new road opening, boats are no longer used as a main form of transport along the Mekong and in the northeast.

Don't miss…

1 **Royal Palace and Silver Pagoda**, page 22.
2 **Tuol Sleng Museum**, page 24.
3 **Bokor Mountain National Park**, page 42.
4 **Kep**, page 44.
5 **Ratanakiri Province**, page 53.
6 **Angkor Wat**, page 67.
7 **The Royal City of Angkor Thom and the Bayon**, page 69.

Numbers relate to map on page 4.

Rail

The UK Foreign Office continues to advise against rail travel in Cambodia, and with its ancient locomotives Cambodian state railways cannot be recommended. The railway is desperately slow, uncomfortable and unreliable. There are two lines out of Phnom Penh: one to Poipet on the Thai border, which goes via Pursat, Battambang and Sisophon; the second, which runs south to Sihanoukville on the coast via Takeo, Kep and Kampot, is not operating at the moment. Check the situation when you arrive.

Road

Over the last few years the road system in Cambodia has dramatically improved. A trunk route of international standards, apart from a few bumpy stretches, from Stung Treng to Koh Kong is due for completion in the near future. Much of the rest of the network is pretty basic and journeys can sometimes be long and laborious. Also, to some parts, such as Ratanakiri, the road is a graded laterite track, unpaved and potholed. In the rainy season expect to be slowed down on many roads to a slithering muddy crawl. The Khmer-American Friendship Highway (Route 4), which runs from Phnom Penh to Sihanoukville, is entirely paved, as is the National Highway 6 between Siem Reap and Phnom Penh. The infamous National Highway 6 between Poipet and Phnom Penh via Siem Reap has also had extensive work, as has National Highway 1. The Japanese in particular have put considerable resources into road and bridge building.

Bus and shared taxi There are buses and shared taxis to most parts of the country. Shared taxis (generally Toyota Camrys) or pickups are usually the quickest and most reliable public transport option. The taxi operators charge a premium for better seats and you can buy yourself more space. It is not uncommon for a taxi to fit 10 people in it, including two sitting on the driver's seat. Fares for riding in the back of the truck are half that for riding in the cab. The Sihanoukville run has an excellent and cheap air-conditioned bus service.

Car hire and taxi A few travel agents and hotels may be able to organize self-drive car hire and most hotels have cars for hire with a driver (US$30-50 per day). There is a limited taxi service in Phnom Penh.

Moto The most popular and sensible option is the motorbike taxi, known as 'moto'. This costs around the same as renting your own machine and with luck you will get a driver

Price codes

Where to stay

$$$$ over US$100 $$$ US$46-100

$$ US$21-45 $ US$20 and under

Price codes refer to the cost of a standard double/twin room in high season.

Restaurants

$$$ over US$12 $$ US$6-12 $ under US$6

Price codes refer to the cost of a two-course meal, not including drinks.

who speaks a bit of English and who knows where he's going. Once you have found a good driver stick with him. Outside Phnom Penh and Siem Reap, do not expect much English from your moto driver.

Motorbike and bicycle hire Motorbikes can be rented from between US$5 and US$8 per day and around US$1 for a bicycle. If riding either a motorbike or a bicycle be aware that the accident fatality rate is very high. This is partly because of the poor condition of many of the vehicles on the road; partly because of the poor roads; and partly because of the horrendously poor driving. If you do rent a motorbike ensure it has a working horn (imperative) and buy some rear-view mirrors so you can keep an eye on the traffic. Wear a helmet (even if using a motodop).

Where to stay in Cambodia

Accommodation standards in Cambodia have greatly improved in recent years. Phnom Penh now has a good network of genuine boutique hotels – arguably they are overpriced and sometimes management can be a bit Fawlty Towers but the bar has certainly been raised. Siem Reap, without doubt, has now become a destination for the upmarket international traveller. The range, depth and quality of accommodation here is of an excellent standard and is on a par with anywhere else in Asia. Even if you travel to some of the less visited towns, family-run Chinese style hotels should now provide hot water, air conditioning and cable TV even if they can't provide first-class service. They are often the best bargains in the country as many of the backpacker places, while very cheap, are hovels.

More expensive hotels have safety boxes in the rooms. In cheaper hotels it is not uncommon for things to be stolen from bedrooms. Most hotels and guesthouses will accept valuables for safekeeping but do keep a close eye on your cash.

Food and drink in Cambodia

There are some good restaurants and things are improving but don't expect Cambodia to be a smaller version of Thailand, or its cuisine even to live up to the standards of Laos. Cambodian food shows clear links with the cuisines of neighbouring countries: Thailand, Vietnam, and to a lesser extent, Laos. The influence of the French colonial period is also in evidence, most clearly in the availability of good French bread. Chinese food is also available owing to strong business ties between Cambodia and China. True Khmer food is difficult to find and much that the Khmers would like to claim as indigenous food is actually of Thai, French or Vietnamese origin. Curries, soups, rice and noodle-based dishes, salads, fried vegetables and sliced meats all feature in Khmer cooking.

Phnom Penh and Siem Reap have the best restaurants with French, Japanese, Italian and Indian food being available. But those who want to sample a range of dishes and get a feel for Khmer cuisine should head for the nearest market where dishes will be cooked to order in a wok – known locally as a chhnang khteak.

International soft drink brands are widely available in Cambodia. Tea is drunk without sugar or milk. Coffee is also served black, or 'crème' with sweetened condensed milk. Bottled water is easy to find, as is local mineral water. Fruit smoothies – known locally as tikalok – are ubiquitous. Soda water with lemon, soda kroch chhmar, is a popular drink.

Local customs and laws

Cambodians are relaxed and easy-going people. Only crass behaviour, such as patting people on the head or invading their homes uninvited, will upset them.

When visiting a temple, dress respectfully (keep bare flesh to a minimum) and take off your hat and shoes. A small donation is often appropriate. Put your legs to one side and try not to point the soles of your feet at anyone or the Buddha image. Females are not to touch monks or sit beside them on public transport.

Cambodians use their traditional greeting – the 'wai' – bowing with their hands held together. As a foreigner shaking hands is perfectly acceptable.

In private homes it is polite to take your shoes off on entering the house and a small present goes down well if you are invited for a meal.

Displays of anger or exasperation are considered unacceptable and therefore reflect very badly on the individual. Accordingly, even in adversity, Khmers (like the Thais) will keep smiling. Displays of affection are also considered embarrassing and should be avoided in public areas. To beckon someone, use your hand with the palm facing downwards. Pointing is rude.

All visitors should dress appropriately and women should avoid wearing short skirts, midriff-baring and cleavage-exposing tops, as this may unwittingly attract undesirable attention and potentially offend some people.

Festivals in Cambodia

There are some 30 public holidays celebrated each year in Cambodia. Most are celebrated with public parades and special events to commemorate the particular holiday. The largest holidays also see many Khmers – although less than used to be the case – firing their guns, to the extent that red tracer fills the sky. Several interesting festivals enliven the Cambodian calendar. The major festivals mark important events in the farming year, determined by seasonal changes in the weather, and are listed below.

1 Jan New Year (public holiday).

7 Jan Victory over Pol Pot (public holiday). Celebration of the fall of the Khmer Rouge.

Jan/Feb Chinese and Vietnamese New Year (movable); Anniversary of the last sermon of Buddha (movable).

8 Mar Women's Day (public holiday). Processions, floats and banners in main towns.

Apr Chaul Chhnam (movable). 3-day celebration, involving the inevitable drenching, to welcome in the new year. A similar festival to Pimai in Laos and Songkran in Thailand.

13-15 Apr Bonn Chaul Chhnam (Cambodian New Year) (public holiday). A 3-day celebration to mark the turn of the year and to show gratitude to the departing demi-god and to welcome the new one. Homes are spring cleaned, householders visit temples and traditional games like boh angkunh and chhoal chhoung are played, and ritual festivities are performed.

17 Apr Independence Day (public holiday). Celebrates the fall of the Lon Nol government.

Apr/May Visak Bauchea (public holiday, movable). Anniversary of Buddha's birth, enlightenment and his Paranirvana (state of final bliss).

9 May Genocide Day (public holiday). To remember the atrocities of the Khmer Rouge. The main ceremony is held at Choeng Ek.

May Royal Ploughing Festival (public holiday, movable). As in Thailand, this marks the beginning of the rainy season and traditionally is meant to alert farmers to the fact that the job of rice cultivation is set to begin. Known as bonn chroat preah nongkoal in Khmer, the ceremony is held on a field close to Phnom Penh.

Jun Anniversary of the Founding of the Revolutionary Armed Forces of Kampuchea and Anniversary of the Founding of the People's Revolutionary Party of Cambodia. Founded in 1951, the main parades and celebrations are in Phnom Penh.

Jul Chol Vassa (movable). The rainy season retreat – a Buddhist Lent – for meditation.

Sep End of Buddhist Lent (movable). In certain areas it is celebrated with boat races. Prachum Ben (public holiday). In remembrance of the dead, offerings are made to the ancestors.

Oct/Nov Water Festival, Bon Om Tuk (public holiday, movable) or Festival of the Reversing Current. To celebrate the movement of the waters out of the Tonlé Sap, boat races are held in Phnom Penh. The festival dates back to the 12th century when King Jayavarman VII and his navy defeated water-borne invaders. Most wats have ceremonial canoes, which are rowed by the monks to summon the Naga King. Boat races extend over 3 days with more then 200 competitors, but the highlight is the evening gala in Phnom Penh when a fleet of boats, studded with lights, row out under the full moon. The festival was only revived in 1990. In addition to celebrating the reversing of the flow of the Tonlé Sap River, this festival marks the onset of the fishing season.

30 Oct-1 Nov King Sihanouk's Birthday (public holiday). Public offices and museums close for about a week and a there is a firework display in Phnom Penh.

Water Festival stampede

Cambodia's annual Bon Om Tuk – or Water Festival – is one of the highlights of the year for Phnom Penh with a giant boat race attracting hundreds of thousands of spectators every November.

Unfortunately, in 2010, the celebrations turned into a horrifying nightmare as over 350 Cambodians were crushed on a bridge in central Phnom Penh during a stampede. Reports at the time stated that thousands of people were trapped on the bridge by sheer weight of numbers while one Phnom Penh Post journalist who was present claimed that the police fired water cannon into the crowd after the authorities feared the bridge might collapse.

However, a terrible panic did erupt on the bridge and some attempted to escape by climbing onto electricity pylons. Cables from these pylons fell onto the crowd and doctors at the scene said that most people died from suffocation and electrocution. An inquiry into these terrible events is still ongoing and the 2011 Phnom Penh boat races were cancelled.

9 Nov Independence Day (public holiday). Marks Cambodia's independence from French colonial rule in 1953.

Dec Half marathon. A half marathon is held at Angkor Wat, surely one of the most spectacular places to work up a sweat.

Shopping in Cambodia

Phnom Penh's markets are highly diverting. Cambodian craftsmanship is excellent and whether you are in search of silverware, kramas – checked cotton scarves – hand-loomed sarongs or bronze buddhas you will find them all in abundance. A great favourite for its range and quality of antiques, jewellery and fabrics is the Psar Tuol Tom Pong (Russian Market). Silverware, gold and gems are available in the Psar Thmei (Central Market). Matmii – ikat – is also commonly found in Cambodia. It may have been an ancient import from Java and is made by tie-dyeing the threads before weaving. It can be bought throughout the country. Other local textile products to look out for are silk scarves bags and traditional wall-hangings. Colourful kramas can be found in local markets across the country and fine woven sarongs in cotton and silk are available in Phnom Penh and Siem Reap. Silk and other textiles products can be bought throughout the country. There has been a strong revival of pottery and ceramics in the last 30 years. Other crafts include bamboo work, wooden panels with carvings of the Ramayana and temple rubbings.

Essentials A-Z

Accident and emergency
Contact the relevant emergency service and your embassy: Ambulance T119/724891, Fire T118, Police T117/112/012-999999. Obtain police/medical records in order to file insurance claims.

Customs and duty free
A reasonable amount of tobacco products and spirits can be taken in without incurring customs duty – roughly 200 cigarettes or the equivalent quantity of tobacco, 1 bottle of liquor and perfume for personal use. Taking any Angkorian era images out of the country is strictly forbidden.

Electricity
Voltage 220. Sockets are usually round 2-pin.

Internet
Cambodia is surprisingly well-connected and most medium-sized to large towns have internet access. Not surprisingly, internet is a lot more expensive in smaller towns, up to a whopping US$5 per hr. In Phnom Penh internet rates are US$1-2 per hr and in Siem Reap should be US$1 per hr or under.

Language
In Cambodia the national language is Khmer Khmer. It is not tonal and the script is derived from the southern Indian alphabet. French is spoken by the older generation who survived the Khmer Rouge era. English is the language of the younger generations. Away from Phnom Penh, Siem Reap and Sihanoukville it can be difficult to communicate with the local population unless you speak Khmer.

Media
Cambodia has a vigorous English-language press that fights bravely for editorial independence and freedom to criticize politicians. The principal English-language newspapers are the fortnightly Phnom Penh Post, which many regard as the best and the Cambodia Daily, published 5 times a week. There are also tourist magazine guides.

Money → *For up-to-date exchange rates, see www.xe.com.*
The riel is the official currency though US dollars are widely accepted and easily exchanged. In Phnom Penh and other towns most goods and services are priced in dollars and there is little need to buy riel. In remote rural areas prices are quoted in riel (except accommodation). Money can be exchanged in banks and hotels. US$ traveller's cheques are easiest to exchange – commission ranges from 1% to 3%. Cash advances on credit cards are available. Credit card facilities are limited but some banks, hotels and restaurants do accept them, mostly in the tourist centres.

ANZ Royal Bank has opened a number of ATMs throughout Phnom Penh. Machines are also now appearing in other towns and a full ATM network should be established in the next couple of years. Most machines give US$ only.

Cost of travelling
The budget traveller will find that a little goes a long way. Numerous guesthouses offer accommodation at around US$3-7 a night. Food-wise, the seriously strapped can easily manage to survive healthily on US$4-5 per day, so an overall daily budget (not allowing for excursions) of US$7-9 should be enough or the really cost-conscious. For the less frugally minded, a daily allowance of US$30 should see you relatively well-housed and fed, while at the upper end of the scale, there are, in Phnom Penh and Siem Reap, plenty of restaurants and hotels for those looking for Cambodian levels

Useful words and phrases

Hello	JOOm ree-up soo-a	Where is the…?	Noev ai nah?
Goodbye	Lee-a hai	Is it far?	Ch'ngai dtay?
Thank you	Or-gOOn	Today	T'ngai ni(h)
How much is …?	…T'lai bpon-mahn?	Tomorrow	Sa-aik
That's expensive	T'lai na(h)	Yesterday	M'Seri mern

of luxury. A mid-range hotel (attached bathroom, hot water and a/c) will normally cost around US$25 per night and a good meal at a restaurant around US$5-10.

Opening hours

Banks Mon-Fri 0800-1600. Some close 1100-1300. Some major branches are open until 1100 on Sat.

Offices Mon-Fri 0730-1130, 1330-1630. Restaurants, cafés and bars Daily from 0700-0800 although some open earlier.

Bars are meant to close at 2400 by law.

Shops Daily from 0800-2000. Some, however, stay open for a further hour or 2, especially in tourist centres. Most markets open daily between 0530/0600-1700.

Police and the law

A vast array of offences are punishable in Cambodia, from minor traffic violations through to possession of drugs. If you are arrested or are having difficulty with the police contact your embassy immediately. As the police only earn approximately US$20 a month, corruption is a problem and contact should be avoided, unless absolutely necessary. Most services, including the provision of police reports, will require paying bribes. Law enforcement is very haphazard, at times completely subjective and justice can be hard to find. Some smaller crimes receive large penalties while perpetrators of greater crimes often get off scot-free.

Post

International service is unpredictable but it is reasonably priced and fairly reliable (at least from Phnom Penh). Only send mail from the GPO in any given town rather than sub POs or mail boxes. Fedex and DHL also offer services.

Safety

Cambodia is not as dangerous as some would have us believe. The country has really moved forward in protecting tourists and violent crime towards visitors is comparatively low. As Phnom Penh has a limited taxi service, travel after dark poses a problem. Stick to moto drivers you know. Women are particularly targeted by bag snatchers. Khmer New Year is known locally as the 'robbery season'. Theft is endemic at this time of year so be on red alert. A common trick around New Year is for robbers to throw water and talcum powder in the eyes of their victim and rob them. Leave your valuables in the hotel safe or hidden in your room.

Outside Phnom Penh safety is not as much of a problem. Visitors should be very cautious when walking in the countryside, however, as landmines and other unexploded ordnance is a ubiquitous hazard. Stick to well worn paths, especially around Siem Reap and when visiting remote temples. There is currently unrest on the border with Thailand around the Preah Vihear temple, check the situation before travelling.

Tax

Airport tax In Cambodia the international departure tax is US$25, domestic tax is US$6. Airport departure taxes are now included in air fares.

Telephone → *Country code +855.*
Landline linkages are so poor in Cambodia that many people and businesses prefer to use mobile phones instead. If you have an unlocked phone and intend to be in the country for a while it is now relatively easy to buy a sim card. This can save you money if you wish to regularly use your phone. International and domestic Cambodian call and sms charges are relatively cheap. There is now an excellent 3G mobile network throughout Cambodia and it can often prove quick than fixed line for internet use. Most mobile phones begin with 01 or 09. The 3-digit prefix included in a 9-digit landline telephone number is the area (province) code. If dialling within a province, dial only the 6-digit number. International calls can be made from most guesthouses, hotels and phone booths but don't anticipate being able to make them outside Phnom Penh, Siem Reap and Sihanoukville. Use public MPTC or Camintel card phone boxes dotted around Phnom Penh to make international calls (cards are usually sold at shops near the booth). International calls are expensive, starting at US$4 per min in Phnom Penh, and more in the provinces. To make an overseas call from Cambodia, dial 007 or 001 + IDD country code + area code minus first 0 + subscriber number. Internet calls are without a doubt the cheapest way to call overseas.

Time
7 hrs ahead of GMT.

Tour operators
Discovery Indochina, 63A Cua Bac St, Hanoi, Vietnam, T+84-4-3716 4132, www.discoveryindochina.com. Organizes private and customized trips throughout Vietnam, Cambodia and Laos.

Tourist information

Government tourism services are minimal at best. The Ministry of Tourism, 3 Monivong Blvd, T023-426876, is not able to provide any useful information or services. The tourism office in Siem Reap is marginally better but will only provide services, such as guides, maps, etc, for a nominal fee. In all cases in Cambodia you are better off going through a private operator for information and price.

Useful websites

www.cambodia-online.com Useful starting point. Tends to be a bit out of date.
www.cambodia.org The Cambodian Information Centre. Wealth of information.
www.embassyofcambodia.org Remarkably good website set up by the Royal Cambodian Embassy in Washington DC. Informative and reasonably up to date.
www.gocambodia.com Useful range of practical information.
www.khmer440.com The forum is very good for bouncing any specific Cambodia questions to the predominantly expat crowd.
www.tourismcambodia.com Cambodia's National Tourism Authority. Good source of general and practical information on travel, visas, accommodation and so on.
www.travel.state.gov Useful information for travellers.

Visas and immigration
E visas

It is now possible to get an e-visa for entry to Cambodia which can be bought, online, before arrival. At present, it is only usable at certain entry and exit points but is likely to be rolled out everywhere in the future. The best thing about this visa is being able to avoid any visa scams etc when arriving at Cambodia's notorious land crossings – at least at those where it can be used.

To apply for an e-visa visit www.mfaic. gov.kh/evisa/. The fee is US$20 plus a US$5 handling fee; it takes 3 working days to process and is valid for 3 months but only for 30 days in Cambodia. There is a list on the website of the entry and exit points where the visa is valid. It can also be extended for 30 days at National Police Immigration Department, Ministry of Interior, 332 Russian Blvd, opposite Phnom Penh International Airport, Phnom Penh, Cambodia. T012-581558, www.immigration. gov.khwww.immigration.gov.kh .

Visas on arrival

Visas for a 30-day stay are available on arrival at Phnom Penh and Siem Reap airport. Tourist visas cost US$20 and your passport must be valid for at least 6 months from the date of entry. You will need a passport photo.

Officially, visas are not available on the Lao border. Many people have reported successfully obtaining visas here but don't rely on it. Travellers using the Lao border should try to arrange visa paperwork in advance in either Phnom Penh, Bangkok or Vientiane. The Cambodian Embassy in Bangkok, 185 Rajdamri Rd, T+66-254 6630, issues visas in 1 day if you apply in the morning, as does the Consulate General in HCMC, Vietnam, 41 Phung Khac Khoan, T+84-8829 2751, and in Hanoi at 71 Tran Hung Dao St, T+84-4942 4788. In both Vietnam and Thailand, travel agencies are normally willing to obtain visas for a small fee. Cambodia has a few missions overseas from which visas can be obtained.

Travellers leaving by land must ensure that their Vietnam visa specifies Moc Bai or Chau Doc as points of entry otherwise they could be turned back. You can apply for a Cambodian visa in HCMC and collect in Hanoi and vice versa.

Visa extensions

Extensions can be obtained at the Department for Foreigners on the road to the airport, T023-581558 (passport photo required). Most travel agents arrange visa extensions for around US$40 for 30 days. Those overstaying their visas are fined US$5 per day, officials at land crossings often try to squeeze out more.

Contents

Cambodia

Phnom Penh

It is not hard to imagine Phnom Penh in its heyday, with wide, shady boulevards, beautiful French buildings and exquisite pagodas. They're still all here but are in a derelict, dust-blown, decaying state surrounded by growing volumes of cars, pickup trucks and motorcyclists. It all leaves you wondering how a city like this works. But it does, somehow.

Phnom Penh is a city of contrasts: East and West, poor and rich, serenity and chaos. Although the city has a reputation as a frontier town, due to drugs, gun ownership and prostitution, a more cosmopolitan character is being forged out of the muck. Monks' saffron robes are once again lending a splash of colour to the capital's streets, following the reinstatement of Buddhism as the national religion in 1989, and stylish restaurants and bars line the riverside. However, the amputees on street corners are a constant reminder of Cambodia's tragic story. Perhaps the one constant in all the turmoil of the past century has been the monarchy – shifting, whimsical, pliant and, indeed, temporarily absent as it may have been. The splendid royal palace, visible to all, was a daily reminder of this ultimate authority whom even the Khmer Rouge had to treat with caution. The royal palace area, with its glittering spires, wats, stupas, national museum and broad green spaces, is perfectly situated alongside the river and is as pivotal to the city as the city is to the country.

Arriving in Phnom Penh

Getting there

Air Phnom Penh International airport lies approximately 10 km west of the city on Road No 4. There are flights to Phnom Penh from Bangkok, Ho Chi Minh City, Vientiane and Siem Reap. A taxi from the airport to town costs US$9 and a moto about US$7. The journey takes between 40 minutes and one hour, although at peak times the roads are often gridlocked, so be prepared for delays in the morning and late afternoon.

Boat and bus It is possible to get to Phnom Penh by boat and bus from Chau Doc in Vietnam and by road crossing at Moc Bai.

Getting around

Fleets of tuk-tuks (*lomphata* in Khmer) provide the nearest thing to taxis in Phnom Penh. Hotels can arrange car hire around town and surrounding areas. Motorbikes are ubiquitous. Most visitors use the local motodops (motorbike taxis where you ride on the back) as a quick, cheap and efficient way of getting around. Be advised that riding a moto can be risky; wear a helmet. There are cyclos too, which undoubtedly appeal to many tourists but for regular journeys they prove to be just too slow and expensive. At present there is no public transport system in Phnom Penh. A bus network has been mooted and there's even talk of a futuristic 'Skytrain' to link the river with the airport but without any concrete plans in place at this stage both projects seem years away. When travelling on any form of public transport in Phnom Penh, be wary of bag snatchers.

Tourist information

Ministry of Tourism ① *3 Monivong Blvd, T023-427130.*

Background

Phnom Penh lies at the confluence of the Sap, Mekong and Bassac rivers and quickly grew into an important commercial centre. Years of war have taken a heavy toll on the city's infrastructure and economy, as well as its inhabitants. Refugees first began to flood in from the countryside in the early 1950s during the First Indochina War and the population grew from 100,000 to 600,000 by the late 1960s. In the early 1970s there was another surge as people streamed in from the countryside again, this time to escape US bombing and guerrilla warfare. On the eve of the Khmer Rouge takeover in 1975, the capital had a population of two million, but soon became a ghost town. On Pol Pot's orders it was forcibly emptied and the townspeople frog-marched into the countryside to work as labourers. Only 45,000 inhabitants were left in the city in 1975 and a large number were soldiers. In 1979, after four years of virtual abandonment, Phnom Penh had a population of a few thousand. People began to drift back following the Vietnamese invasion (1978-1979) and as hopes for peace rose in 1991, the floodgates opened yet again: today the population is approaching one million.

Phnom Penh has undergone an economic revival since the Paris Peace Accord of 1991. Following the 1998 coup, however, there was an exodus of businesses and investors for whom this bloody and futile atrocity was the final straw. The relative stability since the coup has seen a partial revival of confidence but few are willing to risk their capital in long-term investments.

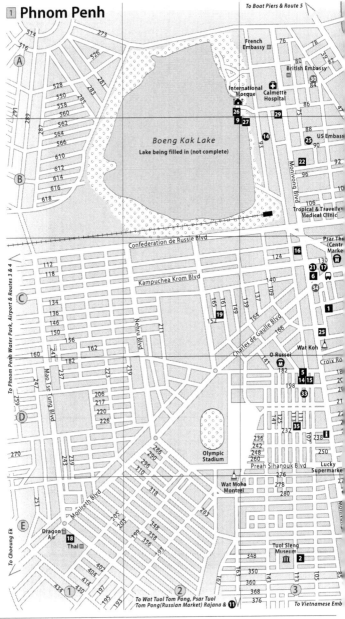

Where to stay 🛏

Almond **23** *E5*
Amber Villa **24** *D4*
Anise **20** *E4*
Aram **28** *D5*
Billabong **1** *C3*
Boddhi Tree **2** *E3*
Capitol **5** *D3*
Diamond **6** *C3*
Flamingo **8** *C4*
Floating Island **9** *B2*
Golden Gate **10** *D4*
Goldiana **3** *E4*
Guesthouse Number 9 **26** *A2*
Happy Guesthouse **14** *D3*
Hello Guesthouse **15** *D3*
Himawari **30** *D5*
Holiday Villa **16** *C3*
Imperial Garden Villa **11** *D5*
Intercontinental **18** *E1*
Juliana **19** *C2*
KIDS **7** *C4*
La Safran La Suite **32** *E4*
Le Royal **22** *B3*

L'Imprévu **13** *E4*
Naga World **33** *D5*
New York **25** *C3*
Number 10 Lakeside
  Guesthouse **27** *B3*
Palm Resort **17** *E4*
Pavilion **38** *D5*
Phnom Penh **29** *A3*
Regent Park **31** *D5*
Royal Guesthouse **39** *C4*
Spring Guesthouse **35** *D3*
Sunway **36** *B3*
Velkommen Inn **40** *B4*
Walkabout **37** *C4*

Restaurants 🍴

Asia Europe Bakery **1** *D3*
Baan Thai **2** *E4*
Comme a la Maison **3** *E4*
Elsewhere **6** *D4*
Garden Centre Café **4** *E4*
Gasolina **8** *F4*
Green Vespa **18** *B4*
Jars of Clay **11** *E3*
Java **10** *D5*
Khmer Surin **12** *E4*
K'nyay **20** *D5*
La Marmite **13** *B4*
Lazy Gecko **14** *B3*
Le Gourmandise Bleu **31** *E3*
Living Room **29** *E4*
Monsoon **35** *B4*
Mount Everest **15** *D4*
Ocean **32** *E4*
Origami **16** *D5*
Peking Canteen **17** *C3*
Pyong Yang **19** *E3*
Romdeng **37** *C4*
Sam Doo **21** *C3*
Shiva Shakti **22** *D4*
Tamarind **23** *D4*
Tell **25** *B3*
Teukei **33** *D3*
The Deli **36** *C4*
The Shop **24** *D4*
Topaz **28** *E4*
Yumi **38** *E3*

Bars & clubs 🍸

Blue Chilli **39** *C4*
Cathouse **26** *C4*
Heart of Darkness **27** *C4*
Manhattan **30** *A3*
Meta House **39** *D5*
Pontoon **40** *B4*
Sharkys **9** *C4*
Zepplin **34** *C3*

➡ **Phnom Penh maps**
1 Phnom Penh, page 20
2 Sisowath Quay, page 24

Places in Phnom Penh → *For listings, see pages 25-35.*

Royal Palace and Silver Pagoda
ⓘ *Entrance on Samdech Sothearos Blvd. Daily 0730-1100, 1400-1700. US$3, plus US$2 for camera or US$5 for video camera.*

The Royal Palace and Silver Pagoda were built mainly by the French in 1866, on the site of the old town. The **Throne Hall**, the main building facing the Victory Gate, was built in 1917 in Khmer style; it has a tiered roof and a 59-m tower, influenced by Angkor's Bayon Temple. The steps leading up to it are protected by multi-headed nagas. It is used for coronations and other official occasions: scenes from the *Ramayana* adorn the ceiling. Inside stand the sacred gong and French-style thrones only used by the sovereign. Above the thrones hangs Preah Maha Svetrachatr, a nine-tiered parasol, which symbolizes heaven. There are two chambers for the king and queen at the back of the hall, which are used only in the week before a coronation when the royal couple are barred from sleeping together. The other adjoining room is used to house the ashes of dead monarchs before they are placed in a royal stupa.

The **Royal Treasury** and the **Napoleon III Pavilion** (summer house), built in 1866, are to the south of the Throne Room. The latter was presented by Napoleon III to his Empress Eugenie as accommodation for the princess during the Suez Canal opening celebrations. She later had it dismantled and dispatched it to Phnom Penh as a gift to the king.

The **Silver Pagoda** is often called the Pagoda of the Emerald Buddha or Wat Preah Keo Morokat after the statue housed here. The wooden temple was originally built by King Norodom in 1892 to enshrine royal ashes and then rebuilt by Sihanouk in 1962. The pagoda's steps are Italian marble, and inside, its floor comprises of more than 5000 silver blocks which together weigh nearly six tonnes. All around are cabinets filled with presents from foreign dignitaries. The pagoda is remarkably intact, having been granted special dispensation by the Khmer Rouge, although 60% of the Khmer treasures were stolen from here. In the centre of the pagoda is a magnificent 17th-century emerald Buddha statue made of Baccarat crystal. In front is a 90-kg golden Buddha studded with 9584 diamonds, dating from 1906. It was made from the jewellery of King Norodom and its vital statistics conform exactly to his – a tradition that can be traced back to the god-kings of Angkor.

National Museum of Cambodia
ⓘ *Entrance is on the corner of streets 13 and 178. Daily 0800-1700. US$3. French- and English-speaking guides are available, mostly excellent.*

The National Museum of Cambodia was built in 1920 and contains a collection of Khmer art – notably sculpture – throughout the ages (although some periods are not represented). Galleries are arranged chronologically in a clockwise direction. Most of the exhibits date from the Angkor period but there are several examples from the pre-Angkor era (that is from the kingdoms of Funan, Chenla and Cham). The collection of Buddhas from the sixth and seventh centuries includes a statue of Krishna Bovardhana found at Angkor Borei showing the freedom and grace of early Khmer sculpture. The chief attraction is probably the pre-Angkorian statue of Harihara, found at Prasat Andat near Kompong Thom. There Is a fragment from a beautiful bronze statue of Vishnu found in the West Baray at Angkor, as well as frescoes and engraved doors.

The riverside and Wat Ounalom

Sisowath Quay is Phnom Penh's Left Bank. A broad pavement runs along the side of the river and on the opposite side of the road a rather splendid assemblage of colonial buildings looks out over the broad expanse of waters. The erstwhile administrative buildings and merchants' houses today form an unbroken chain – almost a mile long – of bars and restaurants, with the odd guesthouse thrown in. While foreign tourist commerce fills the street, the quayside itself is dominated by local Khmer families who stroll and sit in the cool of the evening, served by an army of hawkers.

Phnom Penh's most important wat, **Wat Ounalom**, is north of the national museum, at the junction of Street 154 and Samdech Sothearos Boulevard, facing the Tonlé Sap. The first building on this site was a monastery, built in 1443 to house a hair of the Buddha. Before 1975, more than 500 monks lived at the wat but the Khmer Rouge murdered the Patriarch and did their best to demolish the capital's principal temple. Nonetheless it remains Cambodian Buddhism's headquarters. The complex has been restored since 1979 although its famous library was completely destroyed. The stupa behind the main sanctuary is the oldest part of the wat.

Central Market, Wat Phnom and Boeng Kak Lake

The stunning Central Market (Psar Thmei) is a perfect example of art deco styling and one of Phnom Penh's most beautiful buildings. Inside a labyrinth of stalls and hawkers sell everything from jewellery through to curios. Those who are after a real bargain are better off heading to the Russian Market where items tend to be much cheaper.

Wat Phnom stands on a small hill and is the temple from which the city takes its name. It was built by a wealthy Khmer lady called Penh in 1372. The sanctuary was rebuilt in 1434, 1890, 1894 and 1926. The main entrance is to the east; the steps are guarded by nagas andlions. The principal sanctuary is decorated inside with frescoes depicting scenes from Buddha's life and the *Ramayana*. At the front, on a pedestal, is a statue of the Buddha. There is a statue of Penh inside a small pavilion between the vihara and the stupa, with the latter containing the ashes of King Ponhea Yat (1405-1467). The surrounding park is tranquil and a nice escape from the madness of the city. Monkeys with attitude are in abundance but they tend to fight among themselves.

Boeng Kak Lake was once the main area for budget travellers but the lake has now been partially filled and families are being evicted from this area to make way for new development. The lake was once quite beautiful but close to the guesthouses it began to resemble a floating rubbish tip and with not much lake left it looks more like a canal. In the eyes of the law, the places on the lake are considered 'squatted' so their future is unsure. After the development has been completed some guesthouses may still remain near Boeng Kak but at the time of publication a huge amount of uncertainty remains. Those looking to stay in this area may need to check on arrival for more up-to-date information on whether any accommodation is still available.

Around Independence Monument

South of the Royal Palace, between Street 268 and Preah Sihanouk Boulevard, is the **Independence Monument**. It was built in 1958 to commemorate independence but has now assumed the role of a cenotaph. **Wat Lang Ka**, on the corner of Sihanouk and Norodom boulevards, was another beautiful pagoda that fell victim to Pol Pot's architectural holocaust. Like Wat Ounalom, it was restored in Khmer style on the direction of the Hanoi-backed government in the 1980s. It is a really soothing getaway from city madness and the monks here are particularly friendly. They hold a free meditation session every Monday and Thursday night at 1800; anyone is welcome to join in.

Tuol Sleng Museum (Museum of Genocide)
ⓘ *Street 113, Tue-Sun 0800-1100, 1400-1700; public holidays 0800-1800. US$2; free film at 1000 and 1500.*

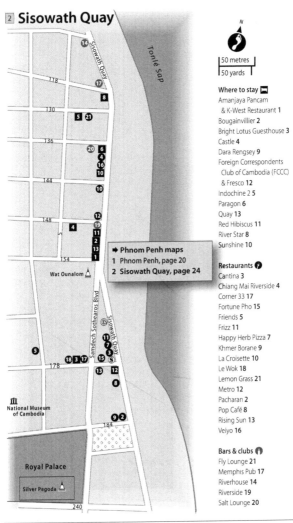

2 Sisowath Quay

N

50 metres
50 yards

Where to stay 🛏
Amanjaya Pancam
  & K-West Restaurant 1
Bougainvillier 2
Bright Lotus Guesthouse 3
Castle 4
Dara Rengsey 9
Foreign Correspondents
  Club of Cambodia (FCCC)
  & Fresco 12
Indochine 2 5
Paragon 6
Quay 13
Red Hibiscus 11
River Star 8
Sunshine 10

Restaurants 🍴
Cantina 3
Chiang Mai Riverside 4
Corner 33 17
Fortune Pho 15
Friends 5
Frizz 11
Happy Herb Pizza 7
Khmer Borane 9
La Croisette 10
Le Wok 18
Lemon Grass 21
Metro 12
Pacharan 2
Pop Café 8
Rising Sun 13
Veiyo 16

Bars & clubs 🍸
Fly Lounge 21
Memphis Pub 17
Riverhouse 14
Riverside 19
Salt Lounge 20

➡ **Phnom Penh maps**
1 Phnom Penh, page 20
2 Sisowath Quay, page 24

After 17 April 1975 the classrooms of Tuol Svay Prey High School became the Khmer Rouge main torture and interrogation centre, known as Security Prison 21 or S-21. More than 20,000 people were taken from S-21 to their executions at Choeung Ek extermination camp, see below. Countless others died under torture and were thrown into mass graves in the school grounds. Only seven prisoners survived because they were sculptors and could turn out countless busts of Pol Pot.

Former US Embassy

The former US Embassy, now home to the Ministry of Fisheries, is at the intersection of Norodom and Mao Tse Tung boulevards. As the Khmer Rouge closed on the city from the north and the south in April 1975, US Ambassador John Gunther Dean pleaded with Secretary of State Henry Kissinger for an urgent airlift of embassy staff. But it was not until the very last minute (just after 1000 on 12 April 1975, with the Khmer Rouge firing mortars from across the Bassac River onto the football pitch near the compound that served as a landing zone) that the last US Marine helicopter left the city. Flight 462, a convoy of military transport helicopters, evacuated the 82 remaining Americans, 159 Cambodians and 35 other foreigners to a US aircraft carrier in the Gulf of Thailand. Their departure was overseen by 360 heavily armed marines. Despite letters to all senior government figures from the ambassador, offering them places on the helicopters, only one, Acting President Saukham Khoy, fled the country. The American airlift was a deathblow to Cambodian morale. Within five days, the Khmer Rouge had taken the city and within hours all senior officials of the former Lon Nol government were executed on the tennis courts of the embassy.

Choeung Ek

① *Southwest on Monireth Blvd, about 15 km from town. US$2. Return trip by moto US$2-5. A shared car (US$10) is more comfortable.*

In a peaceful setting, surrounded by orchards and rice fields, Choeung Ek was the execution ground for the torture victims of Tuol Sleng, the Khmer Rouge extermination centre, S-21 (see above). It is referred to by some as 'The killing fields'. Today a huge glass tower stands on the site, filled with the cracked skulls of men, women and children exhumed from 129 mass graves in the area (which were not discovered until 1980). To date 8985 corpses have been exhumed. Rather disturbingly, rags and crumbling bones still protrude from the mud.

Phnom Penh listings

For hotel and restaurant price codes and other relevant information, see pages 8-9.

● Where to stay

Phnom Penh *p18, maps p20 and p24*
The backpacker area of Boeung Kak Lake is likely to be completely redeveloped in the near future and it is uncertain if any budget accommodation will still be available there. Unfortunately we have decided to delete these listings until the situation has stabilized.

Street 182 offers a selection of cheaper alternatives. The majority of hotels organize airport pickup and most of them for free.
$$$$ Amanjaya Pancam, corner St 154 and Sisowath Quay, T023-219579, www. amanjaya-pancam-hotel.com. Gorgeous rooms full of amenities, beautiful furniture and creative finishing touches. The balconies have some of the best views on the river. Service can be a little ragged – you'll be asked to pay in full when you check-in – but they get enough right to make this probably

the best place by the river. Free Wi-Fi and awesome breakfast are both included in the room rate. Good location. Recommended.

$$$$ Le Royal, St 92, T023-981888, www.raffles-hotelleroyal.com. A wonderful colonial-era hotel built in 1929 that has been superbly renovated by the Raffles Group. The renovation was done tastefully, incorporating many of the original features and something of the old atmosphere. The hotel has excellent bars, restaurants and a delightful tree-lined pool. 2 for 1 cocktails 1600-2000 daily at the Elephant Bar is a must.

$$$$-$$$ The Quay, 277 Sisowath Quay, T023-224894, www.thequayhotel.com. Another hotel from the FCC people set on the riverfront in a remodelled colonial property. It aspires to create a designer feel, which it partly pulls off, although this is slightly undone by a patchy cheap finish. This is compensated by big tubs, flatscreen TVs, a/c, free Wi-Fi and a good location. Also claims to be an 'eco-hotel' though it's not certain if these claims can be substantiated.

$$$$-$$$ Sunway, No 1 St 92, T023-430333, phnompenh.sunwayhotels.com. Overlooking Wat Phnom, this is an adequate hotel in an excellent location. 140 ordinary though well-appointed rooms, including 12 spacious suites, provide comfort complemented by facilities and amenities to cater for the international business and leisure traveller.

$$$ Almond Hotel, 128F Sothearos Bvld. T023-220822, www.almondhotel.com.kh. Stylish, new hotel in upmarket part of town that still offers good value for facilities. The more expensive rooms offer the best deal and come with huge balconies – the cheaper ones have no windows. A/c, en suite and TV throughout. Breakfast and Wi-Fi included.

$$$ Aram, St 244, T023-211376, www.boddhitree.com. Nice little guesthouse tucked away in a small street near the palace. The stylish rooms are a bit miniscule and a tad overpriced.

$$$ Bougainvillier Hotel, 277G Sisowath Quay, T023-220528, www.bougainvillier hotel.com. Lovely riverside boutique hotel, rooms decorated in a very edgy, modern Asian theme, with a/c, safe, cable TV and minibar. Good French restaurant.

$$$ Foreign Correspondents Club of Cambodia (FCCC), 363 Sisowath Quay, T023-210142, www.fcccambodia.com. Known locally as the FCC. 3 decent sized and stylish rooms are available in this well-known Phnom Penh landmark, some with balconies overlooking the river.

$$$ Juliana, No 16, St 152, T023-880530, www.julianahotels.com/phnompenh. A very attractive resort-style hotel with 91 rooms, and decent-sized pool in a secluded garden that provides plenty of shade; several excellent restaurants.

$$$ The Pavilion, 227 St 19, T023-222280, www.thepavilion.asia. A popular and beautiful small, 10-room hotel set in an old French colonial villa. Each room is unique with a/c, en suite and TV. The restaurant also serves decent food. However, we've had several reports of the management abruptly and unceremoniously asking women with children to leave the restaurant.

$$$-$$ Amber Villa, 1a St 57, T023-216303, www.amber-kh.com. This friendly, family-run small hotel is often full so book ahead – rooms include breakfast, laundry and internet – all have a/c, en suite facilities. The best have TV/DVD and balconies.

$$$-$$ Regent Park, 58 Samdech Sothearos Blvd, T023-427131, regentpark@ online.com.kh. The well-designed lobby belies a collection of ordinary rooms and apartment-style suites. Still, it's reasonable value and in a good location. Thai and European restaurant. Price includes breakfast.

$$$-$$ La Safran La Suite, 4 St 282, T023-217646, www.lesafranlasuite.com. Stylish, well-designed and well-lit rooms all with a/c, en suite facilities, internet and cable TV. Arty, designer vibe. Small pool outside. Formerly known as the Scadinavian Hotel.

$$ Billabong, No 5, St 158, T023-223703, www.thebillabonghotel.com. Reasonably new hotel with well-appointed rooms. Breakfast included. Swimming pool, poolside bar and de luxe rooms with balconies overlooking the pool. Internet.

$$ Dara Reang Sey Hotel, 45 Corner St of St 13 and 118 Phsar Chas, T023-428181, www.darareangsey.com. Busy hotel with popular local restaurant downstairs, clean rooms with hot water and some rooms have baths.

$$ Red Hibiscus, No 277c Sisowath Quay, T023-990691. Now owned by the **Bougainvillier Hotel, see above**. Stylish rooms, some with river views, in an excellent location. A/c, en suite and with TV.

$$-$ Anise, 2c St 278, T023-222522, www.anisehotel.com.kh. Excellent value in the heart of a busy area. All rooms are en suite with cable TV and a/c. Pay a little more and you'll get a room with a bath and private balcony. Included in the price is laundry, internet and breakfast. Recommended.

$$-$ Boddhi Tree Umma, No 50, St 113, T016-865445, www.boddhitree.com. A tranquil setting. Lovely old wooden building with guest rooms offering simple amenities, fan only, some rooms have private bathroom. Great gardens and fantastic food. Very reasonable prices.

$$-$ Bright Lotus Guesthouse, No 22 St 178 (near the museum), T023-990446, sammy_lotus@hotmail.com. Fan and a/c rooms with private bathroom and balconies. Restaurant.

$$-$ Golden Gate Hotel, No 9 St 278 (just off St 51), T023-427618, www.goldengatehotels.com. Very popular and comparatively good value for the facilities offered. Clean rooms with TV, fridge, hot water and a/c. Within walking distance to restaurants and bars. Visa/MasterCard.

$$-$ Indochine 2 Hotel, No 28-30 St 130, T023-211525. Great location and good, clean, comfortable rooms.

$$-$ KIDS Guesthouse, No 17A, St 178, T012-410406, ryan@ryanhem.com. Guesthouse of the Khmer Internet Development Service (KIDS) set in a small tropical garden, spotted with a couple of cabana-style internet

kiosks. A couple of rooms are a decent size, quite clean and equipped with a huge fridge. Discount on internet use for guests. Welcoming, safe and free coffee.

$$-$ New York Hotel, 256 Monivong Blvd, T023-214116, www.newyorkhotel.com.kh. The rooms aren't going to set the world on fire but the facilities are good for the price – massage centre, sauna, restaurant and in-room safe.

$$-$ Palm Resort, on Route 1, 5 km out of Phnom Penh, T023-308 6881. Beautiful bungalows surrounded by lush gardens and a very large swimming pool. A/c rooms with very clean bathrooms. Excellent French restaurant. Recommended.

$$-$ Paragon Hotel, 219b Sisowath Quay, T023-222607, info_paragonhotel@yahoo.com. The Paragon gets the simple things right – it's a well-run and friendly hotel. The best and priciest rooms have private balconies overlooking the river. The cheaper rooms at the back are dark but still some of the best value in this part of town. Colour TV, hot water and private shower or bath, a/c or fan. Recommended.

$$-$ Sunshine, No 253 Sisowath Quay, T023-725684. With 50 rooms, a few with a glimpse of the river. Facilities, from a/c to fan, in accordance with price.

$$-$ Velkommen Inn, 23 St 104, T092-177710, www.velkommeninn.com. A friendly Norwegian and his Khmer wife run **Velkommen Inn**. It's located 50 m from Angkor Express and Mekong Express bus stations near the riverside and boat docks and has clean rooms.

$$-$ Walkabout Hotel, corner of St 51 and St 174, T023-211715, www.walkabouthotel.com. A popular Australian-run bar, café and guesthouse. 23 rooms ranging from small with no windows and shared facilities to large with own bathroom and a/c. Rooms and bathrooms are OK but lower-end rooms are a little gloomy and cell-like. 24-hr bar.

$ Capitol, No 14, St 182, T023-217627, www.capitolkh.com. As they say, 'a Phnom Penh institution'. What, in 1991, was a single

guesthouse has expanded to 5 guesthouses all within a stone's throw. All aim at the budget traveller and offer travel services as well as a popular café and internet access. There are a number of other cheap guesthouses in close proximity, such as **Happy Guesthouse** (next door to Capitol Guesthouse) and **Hello Guesthouse** (No 24, 2 St 107) – all about the same ilk.
$ Royal Guesthouse, 91 St 154, hou_heng@yahoo.com. Small family-run guesthouse. Some rooms are much better than others. Ask for the top floor balcony rooms with a/c at US$12; they're worth paying extra for.

⑦ Restaurants

Phnom Penh *p18, maps p20 and p24*
Most places are relatively inexpensive – US$3-6 per head. There are several cheaper cafés along Monivong Blvd, around the lake, Kampuchea Krom Blvd (St 128) in the city centre and along the river. Generally the food in Phnom Penh is good and the restaurants surprisingly refined.
$$$ Bougainvillier Hotel, 277G Sisowath Quay, T023-220528. Upmarket French and Khmer food. Superb foie gras and you can even find truffles here. Fine dining by the river. Recommended.
$$$ Elsewhere, No 175, St 51, T023-211348. An oasis in the middle of the city offering delectable modern Western cuisine. Seats are speckled across wonderful tropical gardens, all topped off by a well-lit pool.
$$$ Foreign Correspondents Club of Cambodia (FCCC), No 363 Sisowath Quay, T023-724014. A Phnom Penh institution that can't be missed. Superb colonial building, 2nd floor bar and restaurant that overlooks the Tonlé Sap. Extensive menu with an international flavour – location excellent, food patchy.
$$$ K-West, Amanjaya Hotel, corner of St 154 and Sisowath Quay, T023-219579. Open 0630-2200. Beautiful, spacious restaurant offering respite from the outside

world. Khmer and European food plus extensive cocktail list. Surprisingly, the prices aren't that expensive considering how upmarket it is. Come early for the divine chocolate mousse – it sells out quickly. Free Wi-Fi. Recommended.
$$$ Metro, corner of Sisowath and St 148. Open 1000-0200. Huge, affordable tapas portions make this a great spot for lunch or dinner. Try the crème brûlée smothered in passion fruit. Free Wi-Fi. Recommended.
$$$ Origami, No 88 Sotheros Blvd, T012-968095. Best Japanese in town, fresh sushi and sashimi. Pricey – one local describes it as where "good things come in very small, expensive packages".
$$$ Pacharan, 389 Sisowath Quay, T023-224394. Open 1100-2300. Excellent Spanish tapas and main courses in a old colonial villa with views across the river and an open kitchen. Stylish Mediterranean feel to it. While the tapas are good value the prices of the main courses are about the highest in town. Part of the FCC empire. Recommended.
$$$ Yi Sang, ground floor of **Almond Hotel** (see Where to stay), daily. Serving up excellent Cantonese food in 3 sittings: 0630-1030 dim sum and noodles, 1130-1400 dim sum and à la carte, 1730-2200 seafood and à la carte – the newish Yi Sang offers some of the best grub in town. Very good quality and great value.
$$$-$$ Corner33, 33 Sothearos Blvd, T092-998850, www.corner33.com. Daily 0700-2200. Set on the upper floors of a building on the corner of St 178, the big sofas and large windows are perfect for views of the palace. Thai and Asian food along with some pasta, coffee and cakes. Free Wi-Fi/internet with coffee.
$$ Baan Thai, No 2, St 306, T023-362991. Open 1130-1400 and 1730-2200. Excellent Thai food and attentive service. Popular restaurant. Garden and old wooden Thai house setting with sit-down cushions.
$$ Boddhi Tree, No 50, St 113, T016-865445, www.boddhitree.com. A delightful

garden setting and perfect for lunch, a snack or a drink. Salads, sandwiches, barbecue chicken. Very good Khmer food.

$$ Cantina, No 347 Sisowath Quay T023-222502. Great Mexican restaurant and bar opened by long-time local identity, Hurley Scroggins III. Fantastic food made with the freshest of ingredients. The restaurant attracts an eclectic crowd and can be a source of great company.

$$ The Deli, near corner of St 178 and Norodom Blvd T012-851234. Great cakes, bread, salads and lunch at this sleek little diner. Sandwich fillings, for the price, are a bit light, though.

$$ Gasolina, 56/58 St 57, T012-373009. Open 1100-late. Huge garden and decent French-inspired food await in this friendly, relaxed restaurant. The owner also arranges t'ai chi and capoeira classes. They normally have a barbecue at the weekends.

$$ Green Vespa, No 95 Sisowath Quay, T012-877228, www.greenvespa.com. Open 0630-late. Serving the best Sunday roast dinners in Cambodia, bacon rolls, fry ups and Cheddar cheese rolls with Branston Pickle. Perfect stop-off if you're a homesick Brit.

$$ Khmer Borane, No 389 Sisowath Quay, T012-290092. Open until 2300. Excellent Khmer restaurant just down from the FCC. Wide selection of very well prepared Khmer and Thai food. Try the Amok.

$$ K'NYAY, 25k Soramit Blvd (St 268), T023-225225, www.knyay.com. Tue-Fri 1200-2100, Sat 0700-2100 and Sun 0700-1500. One of the only places in Phnom Penh that advertises itself as selling vegan food and set in a villa, complete with stylish interior, K'NYAY even has a pretentious name. Unfortunately, despite creating a hip image the food doesn't match. Very average but if you're a veggie, a godsend.

$$ La Croisette, No 241 Sisowath Quay, T023-882221. Authentically French and good value hors d'oeuvres and steak. Good selection of wines.

$$ La Marmite, No 80 St 108 (on the corner with Pasteur), T012-391746. Wed-Mon.

Excellent-value French food – some of the best in town. Extremely large portions.

$$ Le Wok, 33 St 178, T09-821857. Daily 0900-2300. French-inspired Asian food served in this friendly little restaurant located on fashionable street 178. Daily fixed lunch menus and à la carte.

$$ Living Room, No 9 St 306, T023-726139. Tue-Thu 0700-1800 and Fri-Sun 0700-2100. The Japanese owner has done a superlative job at this pleasant hangout spot. The food and coffee is spot-on and the set plates are great value but it's the laid back, calming vibe that is the clincher. There's a purpose-built kids' play area downstairs. Free Wi-Fi if you spend over US$3. Highly recommended.

$$ Mount Everest, 98 Sihanouk Blvd, T023-213821. Open 1000-2300. Has served acclaimed Nepalese and Indian dishes for 5 years, attracting a loyal following. There's also a branch in Siem Reap.

$$ Pop Café, 371 Sisowath Quay, T012-562892. Open 1100-1430 and 1800-2200. Almost perfect, small, Italian restaurant sited next door to the FCC. Owned and managed by Italian expat Giorgio, the food has all the panache you'd expect from an Italian. The home-made lasagne is probably one of the best-value meals in town. Recommended.

$$ Pyong Yang Restaurant, 400 Monivong Blvd, T023-993765. This North Korean restaurant is an all-round experience not to be missed. The food is exceptional but you need to get there before 1900 to get a seat before their nightly show starts. All very bizarre: uniformed, clone-like waitresses double as singers in the nightly show, which later turns into open-mic karaoke.

$$ Rising Sun, No 20, St 178 (just round the corner from the FCC). English restaurant with possibly the best breakfast in town. Enormous roasts and excellent iced coffee.

$$ Romdeng, No 74 St 174 T092-2153 5037, romdeng@mithsamlanh.org. Open 1100-2100. Sister restaurant to Friends (see below), helping out former street kids. Serves just Khmer foods. Watch out for specials like fried tarantula with chilli and garlic.

$$ Veiyo (River Breeze), No 237 Sisowath Quay, T012-847419. Pizza and pasta, along with Thai and Khmer cuisine.

$ Fortune Pho, St 178, just behind the FCC. Open 0800-2100. This small shop offers great Vietnamese, with an authentic and amusingly brusque service.

$ Friends, No 215, St 13, T023-426748. Non-profit restaurant run by street kids being trained in the hospitality industry. The food is delicious and cheap.

$ Frizz, 335 Sisowath Quay, T023-220953. Awesome Khmer food. Friendly service and great location. One of the best spots to eat local food on the riverside. Incredibly cheap as well. Offers cooking classes too. Recommended.

$ Lazy Gecko, St 93, lakeside. Popular, chilled out restaurant/café/bar offering a good selection of sandwiches, burgers and salads in large portions. Good home-cooked Sun roast. Affable owner, Juan, is a good source of information. Selection of new and used books for sale. Good trivia night on Thu.

$ Sam Doo, 56 Kampuchea Krom Blvd, T023-218773. Open until 0200. Late night Chinese food and the best and cheapest dim sum in town.

$ The Shop, No 39, St 240, T012-901964. 0900-1800. Deli and bakery serving sandwiches, juices, fruit teas, salads and lunches.

Cafés and bakeries

Asia Europe Bakery, No 95 Sihanouk Blvd, T012-893177. One of the few Western-style bakery/cafés in the city. Delicious pastries, cakes and excellent breakfast and lunch menu. Recommended.

Fresco, 365 Sisowath Quay, T023-217041. Just underneath the FCC and owned by the same people. They have a wide selection of sandwiches, cakes and pastries of mixed quality and high price.

Garden Centre Café, No 23, St 57, T023-363002. Popular place to go for lunch and breakfast, perhaps not surprisingly, the garden is nice too.

Jars of Clay, No 39 St 155 (beside the Russian Market). Fresh cakes and pastries.

Java, No 56 Sihanouk Blvd. Contenders for best coffee in town. Good use of space, with open-air balcony and pleasant surroundings. Delightful food. Features art and photography exhibitions on a regular basis.

La Gourmandise Bleue, 159 St 278, T023-994019. Tue-Sun 0700-2000. Sweet little French-North African bakery serving up almost perfect cakes and coffee. Famous for its macaroons and also does couscous dishes.

T&C Coffee World, numerous branches – 369 Preah Sihanouk Blvd; Sorya Shopping Centre; 335 Monivong Blvd. Vietnamese-run equivalent of **Starbucks**, but better. Surprisingly good food and very good coffee. Faultless service.

🎵 Bars and clubs

Phnom Penh *p18, maps p20 and p24*
The vast majority of bars in Phnom Penh attract prostitutes.

Blue Chilli, No 36 St 178, T012-566353. Open 1800-late. Gay bar with DJ and dancing. Drag show on Sat.

The Cathouse, corner of St 51 and St 118. Open until 2400. Around since the UNTAC days of the early 1990s and one of the oldest running bars in the city. Not a bad place to have a beer.

Elephant Bar, Le Royal Hotel. Open until 2400. Stylish and elegant bar in Phnom Penh's top hotel, perfect for an evening gin. 2 for 1 happy hour every day with unending supply of nachos, which makes for a cheap night out in sophisticated surroundings. Probably the best drinks in town.

Elsewhere, No 175, St 51. Highly atmospheric, upmarket bar set in garden with illuminated pool. Great cocktails and wine. Very popular with the expats, who have been known to strip off for a dip. Livens up on the last Sat of every month for parties.

Foreign Correspondents Club of Cambodia (FCCC), 363 Sisowath Quay.

Satellite TV, pool, *Bangkok Post* and *The Nation* both available for reading here, happy hour 1700-1900. Perfect location overlooking the river.

Heart of Darkness, No 26, St 51. Reasonable prices, friendly staff and open late. Has been Phnom Penh's most popular hangout for a number of years. Full of prostitutes, but your best bet for a night of dancing. There have been many violent incidents here, so it is advisable to be on your best behaviour in the bar as they do not tolerate any provocation.

Manhattan, in the rather dubious **Holiday International Hotel**, St 84, T023-427402. One of Phnom Penh's biggest discos. Security check and metal detectors at the door prevent you from bringing in small arms.

Memphis Pub, St 118 (off Sisowath Quay). Open till 0200. Small bar off the river. Very loyal following from the NGO crowd. Live rock and blues music from Tue to Sat.

Metro, corner Sisowath and St 148, T023-217517. Open 1000-0200. Serves fine grub and is home to a fabulous bar. Popular with rich Khmers and expats. Recommended.

Riverhouse Lounge, No 6, St 110 Sisowath Quay. Open 1600-0200. Upmarket, cocktail bar and club. Views of the river and airy open balcony space. Live music (Sun) and DJs (Sat).

Riverside Bar, 273a Sisowath Quay. Great riverfront bar. Tasty food. Recommended.

Salt Lounge, No 217, St 136, T012-289905, www.thesaltlounge.com. Funky minimalist bar. Atmospheric and stylish. Gay friendly.

Sharkys, No 126 St 130. "Beware pickpockets and loose women" it warns. Large, plenty of pool tables and food served until late. Quite a 'blokey' hangout.

Talking to a Stranger, No 21 St 294, T012-798530. Great cocktails, relaxed atmosphere. Recommended.

Zepplin Bar aka Rock Bar, No 128, St 136 (just off Monivong beside the Central Market), open until late. Hole in the wall bar owned by a Taiwanese man named Joon who has more than 1000

records for customers to choose from. Cheap beer and spirits.

😃 Entertainment

Phnom Penh *p18, maps p20 and p24*
Pick up a copy of the *Cambodia Daily* and check out the back page, it details up-and-coming events.

Dance
National Museum of Cambodia, St 70. Folk and national dances are performed by the National Dance group as well as shadow puppets and circus. Fri and Sat 1930, US$4.

Live music
Memphis Pub, St 118 (off Sisowath Quay), open until 0200. Small bar off the river, very loyal following from the NGO crowd. Live rock and blues music from Tue-Sat.

Riverhouse Lounge, No 6, St 110 (Sisowath Quay). Usually has a guest DJ on the weekends and live jazz on Tue and Sun.

☉ Shopping

Phnom Penh *p18, maps p20 and p24*
Art galleries Reyum Institute of Arts and Culture, No 4, St 178, T023-217149, www.reyum.org. Open 0800-1800. This is a great place to start for those interested in Cambodian modern art. Some world-class artists have been mentored and exhibit here.

Handicrafts Many non-profit organizations have opened stores to help train or rehabilitate some of the country's under-privileged.
Bare Necessities, No 46 St 322, T023-996664. Selling a range of bras and underwear which fit Western sizes, from maternity to sporty to sexy. A social enterprise raising money to support awareness and treatment of breast cancer for poor, rural Cambodian women.

Disabled Handicrafts Promotion Association, No 317, St 63. Handicrafts and jewellery made by people with disabilities.
Nyemo, No 71 St 240 between St 63 and Monivong Boulevard, www.nyemo.com.
The National Centre for Disabled People, 3 Norodom, T023-210140. Great store with handicrafts such as pillow cases, tapestries and bags made by people with disabilities.
Orange River, 361 Sisowath Quay (under FCCC), T023-214594, has a selection of beautifully designed decorative items and a very good stock of fabrics and silks which will leave many wishing for more luggage allowance. Pricier than most other stores.
Rajana, No 170, St 450, next to the Russian Market. Traditional crafts.
Silk & Pepper, 33 St 178 (next door to Le Wok, see Restaurants). Contemporary, sleek, Khmer-inspired fashions and silks, Also sells Kampot pepper in little china pots.

Markets Psar Thmei (Central Covered Market), just off Monivong Blvd, distinguished by its central art deco dome (built 1937), is mostly full of stalls selling silver and gold jewellery.
Tuol Tom Pong, between St 155 and St 163 to east and west, and St 440 and St 450 to north and south. Known to many as the Russian Market. Sell huge range of goods, fabrics and an immense variety of tobacco – an excellent place for buying souvenirs, especially silk. Most things at this market are about half the price of the Central Market.

Shopping centres Sorya Shopping Centre, St 63, besides the Central Market. 7-floor, a/c shopping centre. It even has a skating rink.

Silverware and jewellery Old silver boxes, belts, antique jewellery along Monivong Blvd (the main thoroughfare), Samdech Sothearos Blvd just north of St 184, has a good cluster of silver shops.

Supermarkets Sharky Mart, No 124, St 130 (below **Sharkys Bar**), T023-990303. 24-hr convenience store.

⊙ What to do

Phnom Penh *p18, maps p20 and p24*
Cookery courses
Cambodia Cooking Class, No 14, St 285, T023-882314, www.cambodia-cooking-class.com.

Language classes
The Khmer School of Language, No 529, St 454, Tuol Tumpung 2, Chamcar Morn, T023-213047, www.camb comm.org.uk/ksl.

Tour operators
Asia Pacific Travel, 19-20 EO, St 371, T023-884432, www.angkortravelcambodia.com. Operates tours throughout the region.
Asian Trails, No 22, St 294, Sangkat Boeng Keng Kong I, Khan Chamkarmorn, PO Box 621, T023-216555, www.asiantrails.travel. Offers a broad selection of tours: Angkor, river cruises, remote tours, biking trips.
Capitol Tours, No 14AE0, St 182 (see **Capitol Guesthouse**), T023-217627, www.bigpond. com.kh/users/capitol. Cheap tours around Phnom Penh's main sites and tours around the country. Targeted at budget travellers.
Exotissimo Travel, 6th floor, SSN Center No 66 Norodom Blvd, T023-218948, www.exotissimo.com. Wide range of day trips and classic tours covering mainstream destinations.
Luxury Travel, 19-20 Eo, St 371, (off Maida St), T023-884432, www.luxurytravelvietnam. com. Asian specialist in luxury private guided and fully bespoke holidays in Vietnam, Laos, Cambodia, Myanmar and Thailand.
PTM Tours, No 333B Monivong Blvd, T023-219161, www.ptm-travel.com. Reasonably priced package tours to Angkor and around Phnom Penh. Offers cheap hotel reservations.
RTR Tours, No 54E Charles de Gaulle Blvd, T023-210468, www.rtrtours.com.kh. Tours and travel services. Friendly and helpful.

Phnom Penh *p18, maps p20 and p24*
Air

Siem Reap Airways and new national carrier, Cambodia Angkor Air have connections with Siem Reap. Book in advance.

Airline offices Most airline offices are open Mon-Fri 0800-1700, Sat 0800-1200. AirAsia, Room T6 Phnom Penh Airport, T023-890035, www.airasia.com. Asiana Airlines, Room A16, Domestic Arrival Terminal, Phnom Penh Airport, T023-890441, www.flyasiana. com. Bangkok/Siem Reap Airways, No 61A St 214, T023-722545, www.bangkokair. com. China Airlines, 32 Norodom, T023-222056, www.china-airlines.com. Cambodia Angkor Air, 1-2/294, Mao Tse Tung, T023-6666786, www.cambodiaangkorair.com. Dragon Air, Unit A3, 168 Monireth Blvd, T023-424300, www.dragonair.com. Jet Star Asia, 333b Monivong, T023-220909, www. jetstarasia.com. Lao Airlines, 111 Sihanouk Blvd, T023-222956. Malaysian Airlines, 35-37 Samdech Pan, St 214, T023-218923, www.malaysiaairlines.com. Silk Air, 219B Himawari Hotel, T023-426806, www.silkair. net. Thai T023-214359, www.thaiairways. com. Vietnam Airlines, No 41 St 214, T023-990840, www.vietnamairlines.com.vn.

Bicycle

Hire from guesthouses for about US$1 per day. Cycling is probably the best way to explore the city as it's mostly flat.

Boat

Fast boats to **Siem Reap** depart from the tourist boat dock on Sisowath Quay at the end of 106 St. Ferries leave from wharves on the river north of the Japanese Friendship Bridge. Fast boat connections (5 hrs) with **Siem Reap**, US$35 1 way. All boats leave early, 0700 or earlier. Most hotels will supply ferry tickets.

Bus

Most buses leave southwest of Psar Thmei (Central Market) by the Shell petrol station. All the companies mentioned here run a service between **Siem Reap** and **Phnom Penh**. Capitol Tours, T023-217627, departs from its terminal, No 14, St 182. GST, T012-895550, departs from the southwest corner of the Central Market (corner of St 142). Phnom Penh Public Transport Co (formerly Ho Wah Genting Bus Company), T023-210359, departs from Charles de Gaulle Blvd, near the Central Market. To **Kratie**, 1 bus per day (US$4); Capitol Tours runs a bus to **Kampot**, 0700 and 1300, US$3.50. There are also frequent departures from the Central Market (Psar Thmei) bus terminal. **Phnom Penh Bus Co** to **Sihanoukville**, 5 times daily. GST buses leave 4 times daily, 4 hrs. To **Siem Reap**, see page 74. Virak Buntham Express Travel, Street 106, on the riverfront opposite the Night Market, T012-322302, run buses to and from **Koh Kong**, 0800. To **Stung Treng** the Soyra bus, Central Bus Station, T023-210359, leaves Phnom Penh at 0715, US$10. The Soyra bus also leaves for **Banlung, Ratanakiri** at 0700.

Buses from **Phnom Penh** to **Ho Chi Minh City** depart daily (Phnom Penh Public Transport Co, Capitol Tour, Soyra, Mekong Express), 8 hrs, US$9-12 per 1-way ticket. The Soyra bus company and Mekong Express run a daily bus to **Bangkok** from **Phnom Penh**, 0630 and 0730, US$9. The Soyra bus company also run frequent routes to **Laos** and leaves **Phnom Penh** for **Pakse** every morning at 0645, US$27.

Car

Car Rental, T012-950950. Chauffeur-driven cars are available at most hotels from US$25 per day upwards. Several travel agents will also hire cars. Prices increase if you're venturing out of town.

Mr Vanny, a local English-speaking guide and driver, offers an excellent fast and safe service to pretty much anywhere in Cambodia – T09-285 0989/T01-197 7328.

Cyclo

Plentiful but slow. Fares can be bargained down but are not that cheap – a short journey should be no more than 1000 riel. A few cyclo drivers speak English or French. They are most likely to be found loitering around the big hotels and can also be hired for the day (around US$5).

Moto

'Motodops' are 50-100cc motorbike taxis and the fastest way to get around Phnom Penh. Standard cost per journey is around US$0.50 for a short hop but expect to pay double after dark. If you find a good, English-speaking moto driver, hang on to him and he can be yours for US$8-10 per day.

Shared taxi

These are either Toyota pickups or saloons. For the pickups the fare depends upon whether you wish to sit inside or in the open; vehicles depart when the driver has enough fares. **Psar Chbam Pao**, just over Monivong Bridge on Route 1, for **Vietnam**. For **Sihanoukville** and **Siem Riep**, take a shared taxi from the Central Market (Psar Thmei). Leave early 0500-0600. Shared taxi to **Kampot** takes 2-3 hrs, US$4, leaving from Doeum Kor Market on Mao Tse Tung Blvd.

Taxi

There are only a few taxis in Phnom Penh. It is possible to get a taxi into town from the airport and 1 or 2 taxi companies can be reached by telephone but expect to see no cabs cruising and no meter taxis. Taxi Vantha, T012-855000/T023-982542, 24 hrs.

Phnom Penh hotels will organize private taxis to **Sihanoukville** for around US$40-50. Global Taxi, T011-311888, T092 889962, are Phnom Penh's 1st meter taxi service. US$1 at flagfall for 1st 2 km then US$0.10 per km. On call 24/7.

Train

The railway station is a recently restored, fine old 1930s art deco French edifice. These days the station's main function is to provide a place for the homeless to sleep. The station is on Monivong Blvd between 106 and 108 streets. There are 2 lines: the southern line to **Sihanoukville** and the northern line to **Battambang**. At the time of publication there were no rail services running in Cambodia though plans are emerging for routes to reopen.

● Directory

Phnom Penh *p18, maps p20 and p24*
Banks ANZ Royal Bank, Russian Blvd, 20 Kramuon Sar (corner of street 67), has opened ATMs throughout Phnom Penh; near the Independence Monument; 265 Sisowath Quay. Canadia Bank, No 126 Charles de Gaulle Blvd, T023-214668; 265-269 Ang Duong St, T023-215286. Cash advances on credit cards. Cambodia Commercial Bank (CCB), No 130 Monivong Blvd (close to the Central Market), T023-426208. Cash advance on credit cards, TCs and currency exchange. Union Commercial Bank (UCB), No 61, St 130, T023-724931. Most banking services, charges no commission on credit card cash advances.
Embassies and consulates See http://embassy.goabroad.com for foreign embassies and consulates in Cambodia.
Emergency services Ambulance, T119 (from 023 phones) or T023-723840. Fire, T118 (from 023 phones) or T023-723555 or T012-786693. Police, T117, T112 (from 023 phones) and T012-999999 or for tourist police T097-7780002. To report child abuse, T023-720555.
Immigration Opposite the international airport. Visa extensions, photograph required, 1 month US$30. **Internet** Nearly every café, restaurant, guesthouse and hotel now has free Wi-Fi. In addition, Phnom Penh has an excellent mobile 3G network which can often be quicker than fixed line, cable internet. Internet cafés/shops are also extremely cheap and ubiquitous. Rates can be as low as US$0.50 per hr although in many places they are higher. **Medical services** It is highly advisable to try and get to Bangkok if you are seriously ill or have injured yourself as Cambodia's medical services are not up to scratch. Bumrungrad Hospital Office, 113 Mao Tse Tung Blvd, T023-221103, is the local service office for the private hospital in Bangkok. Calmette Hospital, 3 Monivong Blvd, T023-426948, is generally considered the best, 24-hr emergency. Tropical and Travellers Medical Clinic, No 88 St 108, T023-306802. English doctor. Pharmacy de la Gare, 81 Monivong Blvd, T023-526855. **Post office** Main post office, St 13, possible to make international telephone calls from here.

Southern Cambodia

With the opening of the Vietnamese border near Kampot at Ha Tien, southern Cambodia is now firmly grasping its tourist potential as a staging post for overland travellers. Yet, in many ways it manages to encompass the worst and best of what tourism can offer to a developing country such as Cambodia. Take Sihanoukville, which not so long ago was a sleepy port offering idyllic beaches. Now, with human waste pouring directly into the sea from dozens of generic backpacker shanty bars and flophouses, this town could almost offer a textbook study in environmental catastrophe.

Travel down the coast to Kep and Kampot, and things couldn't be more different. An old French trading port overlooking the Prek Kamping Bay River and framed by the Elephant Mountains, low-key Kampot is filled with decrepit dusty charm. Just outside Kampot is Kep, the resort of choice for France's colonial elite, which is now slowly reasserting its position as a place for rest and recuperation. Don't go to Kep expecting wild nights or even a great beach, but perfect views, good seafood and serenity are on offer here.

Northwest from Sihanoukville is Koh Kong province, a vast and untamed expanse of jungle that smothers the stunning Cardamom Mountain range in a thick green blanket. There's a sealed road through here linking Sihanoukville with Thailand. With logging companies waiting in the wings, this area is facing an uncertain future.

Sihanoukville → *For listings, see pages 44-50.*

If Sihanoukville was being tended with care it would occupy a lovely site on a small peninsula whose knobbly head juts out into the Gulf of Thailand. The first-rate beaches, clean waters, trees and invigorating breezes are slowly being replaced with human effluvia, piles of rubbish and nasty flophouses. Cambodia's beaches could be comparable to those in Thailand but are slowly being horribly degraded. Most people head for beaches close to the town which, starting from the north, are Victory, Independence, Sokha, Ochheauteal and, a little further out, Otres. Sihanoukville's layout is unusual, with the 'town' itself acting as a satellite to the roughly equidistant main beaches. The urban area is pretty scattered and has the distinct feel of a place developing on an ad hoc basis.

Arriving in Sihanoukville
There are regular departures from Phnom Penh in comfortable, well-maintained, air-conditioned coaches, costing US$3-5 with the luxury Mekong Express service costing US$7. Buses generally leave every 30 minutes from 0700 until 1330. Taxis cost US$40-50. There is now a fledgling bus service linking Sihanoukville to Kampot and Kep, but this can depend on season and demand making the journey along the shoreline not always the easiest (though there are plentiful buses from Phnom Penh to these coastal jewels). You can also travel to Koh Kong via the new road from Sihanoukville or Hat Lek, Thailand. With the new road and bridges finally completed the boat from Sihanoukville to Koh Kong has disappeared; there is now a daily bus (US$10). Departing from Sihanoukville there are shared taxis to Kampot and Phnom Penh at around 0700-0800, US$5-6. You can travel to Koh Kong from Sihanoukville or Hat Lek, Thailand. For getting around in Sihanoukville most people use motodops (US$0.25-1 depending on distance) or tuk-tuks, which can be rented by the day. It is possible to rent motorcycles though there do seem to be periodic bans for tourists using these. If a ban is in force we have heard reports of fines and even motorcycles being seized. As anywhere else in the world if you rent a motorcycle wear a helmet. ➧➧ *See Transport, page 49.*

Background
Sihanoukville, or Kompong Som as it is called during the periods the king is in exile or otherwise 'out of office', was founded in 1964 by Prince Sihanouk to be the nation's sole deep-water port. It is also the country's prime seaside resort. In its short history it has crammed in as much excitement as most seaside towns see in a century – but not of the sort that resorts tend to encourage. Sihanoukville was used as a strategic transit point for weapons used in fighting the US, during the Vietnam War. In 1975, the US bombed the town when the Khmer Rouge seized the container ship *SS Mayaguez*.

Sihanoukville has now turned a corner, however, and with rapid development has firmly secured its place in Cambodia's 'tourism triangle', alongside Phnom Penh and Angkor Wat. Not much of this development is sustainable and incredibly tacky and overpriced resorts have already being built. While a liberal attitude towards the smoking of marijuana attracts a youthful crowd, no amount of intoxicants can cover up the fact that Sihanoukville is rapidly becoming an environmental stain on this already horribly scarred country. By late 2009 massive offshore sand-dredging was also having an impact on this fragile coastline; the beaches here were slowly being eroded with high tides swamping many of the beachside bars and restaurants. If it all becomes too much there is the coastal Preah Sihanouk 'Ream' National Park close by.

Sihanoukville

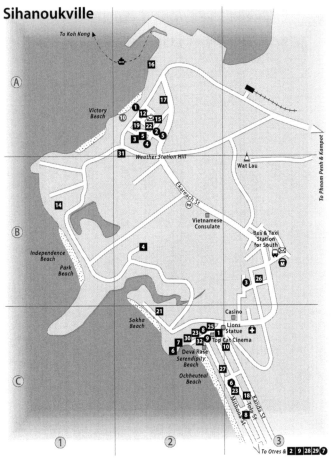

200 metres
200 yards

Where to stay 🛏
Beach Rd 1 *C2*
Bungalow Village 3 *A2*
Castaways (Otres) 2 *C3*
Chez Claude 4 *B2*
Chez Mari-yan 5 *A2*
Cloud 9 6 *C2*

Coasters Guesthouse 7 *C2*
Crystal 8 *C3*
Golden Sand 10 *C*
GST Guesthouse 27 *C2*
Holiday Palace & Casino 12 *A2*
Independence 14 *B1*
Mealy Chenda 15 *A2*
Mean Mean (Otres) 9 *C3*
Monkey Republic 23 *C2*
Motel 7 24 *C3*
New Beach 16 *A2*
Nika 17 *A2*
Ocean Front (Otres) 28 *C3*

Orchidée 18 *C3*
Reef Resort 25 *C2*
Sakal Bungalows 19 *A2*
Sea Garden (Otres) 29 *A2*
Seahorse 30 *C2*
Seaside 20 *C3*
Snake House 31 *A2*
Sokha Beach Resort 21 *C2*
Sunset Garden Inn 22 *A2*
Utopia 32 *C2*
Zen Garden 26 *B3*

Restaurants 🍴
Cabbage Garden 3 *B3*
Cantina del Mar Otres 7 *C3*
Chhner Molop Chrey 1 *A2*
Corner Bar 2 *A2*
Escape 9 *C2*
Indian Curry Pot 5 *A2*
Les Feuilles 6 *C3*
Mick & Craig's 8 *C2*
Paillote 4 *A2*

Bars & clubs 🎵
Airport 10 *A2*

Places in Sihanoukville
Victory Beach is a thin, 2-km-long beach on the north of the peninsula, just down from the port, and at its extremes offers reasonably secluded beaches. Beach hawkers are ubiquitous and outnumber tourists at a ratio of about three to one. The area does afford a good sunset view, however. **Independence Beach** was at one time the sole preserve of the once bombed and charred – and now beautifully restored – **Independence Hotel**. The location of the hotel is magnificent and the grounds are a reminder of the place's former grandeur. With the restoration of this sleek hotel complete, its re-opening will do a lot to revive Independence Beach's fortunes. **Sokha Beach** is arguably Sihanoukville's most beautiful beach. The shore laps around a 1-km arc and even though the large **Sokha Beach Resort** has taken up residence it is very rare to see more than a handful of people on the beach. It is stunning and relatively hassle-free. **Ochheuteal Beach** lies to the south and, bizarrely, is the most popular with hordes of backpackers. What was once a sparkling stretch of white sand has been reduced to an unending dustbin of rickety, badly planned budget bars, restaurants and accommodation. Several of these places have now been cleared out and this stretch of beach is attempting to move upmarket. Along the beach front road here keep a look out for Hun Sen's massive and impregnable residence. Watch your stuff as theft is also common here.The beach commonly referred to as **Serendipity Beach** is at the very north end of Ochheauteal and is basically Ochheauteal-like. This little strand has gained flavour with travellers due in part to being the first beach in Sihanoukville to offer a wide range of budget accommodation. At the time of publication, the many guesthouses and restaurants lining the shore of Serendipity and the extended Ochheauteal Beach area were at the centre of a land dispute with developers hankering to clear the budget accommodation to make way for large Thai-style resorts.

Otres Beach is a couple of kilometres south of Ochheauteal and is, at least for the moment, relatively quiet and undeveloped. The stretch of sand here is probably Sihanoukville's longest and it is easy to find a spot for yourself. There are now a number of budget guesthouses opening up should you wish to stay here (see Where to stay, page 45). To reach Otres you'll need to take a moto or tuk-tuk (US$3-4). Be careful of walking the long road out here or passing through the local fishing village, as several tourists have been robbed, threatened and even a stabbing has been reported.

Preah Sihanouk 'Ream' National Park
ⓘ *T012-875096, daily 0700-1715. Boat trip US$30 for 4 people. Nature trek with a guide (3-5 hrs), US$5 per person.*
This beautiful park is a short 30-minute drive from Sihanoukville, hugging the coastline of the Gulf of Thailand. It includes two islands and covers 21,000 ha of beach, mangrove swamp, offshore coral reef and the Prek Tuk Sap Estuary. Samba deer, endangered civet species, porcupines and pangolin are said to inhabit the park, as well as dolphins. To arrange a guided tour visit the park office or arrange one through a guesthouse in Sihanoukville.

Koh Kong and around → *For listings, see pages 44-50.*

Dusty Koh Kong is better known for its brothels, casinos and 'Wild West' atmosphere than for lying at the heart of a protected area with national park status (granted by Royal Decree in 1993). It is also often confused with its beautiful offshore namesake Koh Kong Island. The town is also reputed to have the highest incidence of HIV infection of anywhere in

Sihanoukville's islands

More than 20 beautiful islands and pristine coral reefs lie off Sihanoukville's coastline. Most of the islands are uninhabited except Koh Russei (Bamboo Island), Koh Rong Salaam and a few others that contain small fishing villages.

Diving and snorkelling around the islands is pretty good. The coast offers an abundance of marine life including star fish, sea anemones, lobsters and sponge and brain coral. Larger creatures such as stingrays, angel fish, groupers, barracuda, moray eels and giant clams are ubiquitous. Baby whale sharks and reef sharks also roam the waters. More elusive are the black dolphins, pink dolphins, common dolphins and bottle-nosed dolphins but they are sighted from time to time. It is believed that further afield (closer to Koh Kong) are a family of dugongs (sea cows). No one has sighted these rare creatures except for one hotel owner who sadly saw a dugong head for sale in Sihanoukville's market.

The islands are divided into three separate groups: the Kampong Som Group, the Ream Group and the Royal Islands. The Kampong Som Islands are the closest to Sihanoukville and have quite good beaches. Here the visibility stretches up to 40 m. Koh Pos is the closest island to Sihanoukville, located just 800 m from Victory Beach. Most people prefer Koh Koang Kang also known as Koh Thas, which is 45 minutes from shore. This island has two beautiful beaches (with one named after Elvis) and the added attraction of shallow rocky reefs, teeming with wildlife, which are perfect for snorkelling. More rocky reefs and shallow water can be found at the Rong Islands. Koh Rong is about two hours west of Sihanoukville and has a stunning, 5-km-long sand beach (on the southwest side of the island). To the south of the Koh Rong is Koh Rong Salaam, a smaller island that is widely considered Cambodia's most beautiful. There are nine fantastic beaches spread across this island and on the east coast, a lovely heart-shaped bay. It takes about 2½ hours to get to Koh Rong from Sihanoukville. Koh Kok, a small island off Koh Rong Salaam, is one of the firm favourite dive sites, warranting the nickname 'the garden' and takes 1¾ hours to get there.

During winter (November to February) the Ream Islands are the best group to visit as they are more sheltered than some of the other islands but they are a lot further out.

Cambodia and is a haven for members of the Thai mafia trying to keep their heads down and launder large sums of money through the casino. The place is only really used by travellers as a transit stop on the way to and from Thailand or two of the most scenic places in Cambodia – Koh Kong Island and the Cardamom Mountains. Due to its border location most people in Koh Kong will accept Thai baht as well as the usual US dollars and Cambodian riel.

Central Cardamoms Protected Forest

① *The area remains relatively inaccessible but over the next few years it is anticipated that ecotourism operators will flock to the area. For now, it is best to make short trips into the park as the area is sparsely populated and heavily mined (so stay on clearly marked paths). Take a motorbike (with an experienced rider) or a boat. The latter option is more convenient in Koh*

The Ream Islands encompass those islands just off the Ream coast: Prek Mo Peam and Prek Toek Sap, which don't offer the clearest waters. The islands of Koh Khteah, Koh Tres, Koh Chraloh and Koh Ta Kiev are best for snorkelling. Giant mussels can be seen on the north side of Koh Ta Kiev island. Some 50 km out are the outer Ream Islands which, without a doubt, offer the best diving in the area. The coral in these islands though has started to deteriorate and is now developing a fair bit of algae. Kondor Reef, 75 km west of Sihanoukville, is a favorite diving spot. A Chinese junk filled with gold and other precious treasures is believed to have sunk hundreds of years ago on the reef and famous underwater treasure hunter, Michael Archer, has thoroughly searched the site but no one can confirm whether he struck gold.

Koh Tang, Koh Prins and Paulo Wai are seven hours away to the southwest. These islands are believed to have visibility that stretches for 40 m and are teeming with marine life; they are recommended as some of the best dive sites. It is believed that Koh Prins once had a modern shipwreck and sunken US helicopter but underwater scavengers looking for steel and US MIA guys have completely cleared the area. Large schools of yellow fin tuna are known to inhabit the island's surrounding waters. Koh Tang is worth a visit but is quite far from the mainland so an overnight stay on board might be required. Many local dive experts believe Koh Tang represents the future of Cambodia's diving. The island became infamous in May 1975 when the US ship SS Mayaguez was seized by the Khmer Rouge just off here. The area surrounding Paulo Wai is not frequently explored, so most of the coral reefs are still in pristine condition.

Closer to Thailand lies Koh Sdach (King's Island), a stop off on the boat ride between Sihanoukville and Koh Kong. This undeveloped island is home to about 4000 people, mostly fishing families. The beaches are a bit rocky but there is some fabulous snorkelling. At the time of publication a guesthouse was being built on the island.

The Cambodian diving industry is still in its fledgling years; most of the islands and reefs are still in relatively pristine condition and the opportunities to explore unchartered waters limitless.

Some of the islands mentioned above now have guesthouses and hotels, see page 45 for details.

see page 45 for details.

Kong. There are usually several men with boats willing to take the trip down the Mohaundait Rapids, cutting through the jungled hills and wilderness of the Cardamoms. The cost of the trip is between US$25-30.

In 2002, the government announced the creation of the **Central Cardamoms Protected Forest**, a 402,000-ha area in Cambodia's Central Cardamom Mountains. With two other wildlife sanctuaries bordering the park, the total land under protection is 990,000 ha – the largest, most pristine wilderness in mainland Southeast Asia. The extended national park reaches widely across the country, running through the provinces of Koh Kong, Pursat, Kompong Speu and Battambang. Considering that Cambodia has been severely deforested and seen its wildlife hunted to near-extinction, this park represents a good opportunity for the country to regenerate flora and fauna. The Cardamoms are home to most of Cambodia's large mammals and half of the country's birds, reptiles and amphibians. The mountains have retained large populations of the region's most rare and endangered animals, such as the Indochinese tigers, Asian elephants and sun bears. Globally threatened species like the pileated gibbon and the critically endangered Siamese crocodile, which has its only known wild breeding population here, exist. Environmental surveyors have identified 30 large mammal species, 30 small mammal species, more than 500 bird species, 64 reptile species and 30 amphibian species. Conservationists are predicting they will discover other animals that have disappeared elsewhere in the region such as the Sumatran rhinoceros. With virgin jungles, waterfalls, rivers and rapids this area has a huge untapped ecotourism potential. However, tourist services to the area are still quite limited.

Koh Kong Island

① About 1-1½ hrs by boat from Koh Kong town. Boats from town usually charge ฿1000 per round trip. Koh Kong Divers offer diving and snorkelling trips to Koh Kong, see page 49.

The island (often called Koh Kong Krau) is arguably one of Cambodia's best. There are six white powdery beaches each stretching kilometre after kilometre, while a canopy of coconut trees shade the glassy-smooth aqua waters. It's a truly stunning part of the country and has been ear-marked by the government for further development, so go now, while it's still a little utopia. There are a few frisky dolphin pods that crop up from time to time. Their intermittent appearances usually take place in the morning and in the late afternoon. You could feasibly camp on the island though would likely need to bring all supplies with you, including drinking water.

Kampot and around → For listings, see pages 44-50.

Kampot is a charming riverside town that was established in the 19th century by the French. The town lies at the base of the Elephant Mountain Range, 5 km inland on the river Prek Thom and was for a long time the gateway to the beach resort at Kep (see page 44). On one side of the river are tree-lined streets, crumbling mustard yellow French shop fronts and a sleepy atmosphere, while on the other side you will find locals working in the salt pans. The town has the feel of another era – with a dabbling of Chinese architecture and overall French colonial influence – which, with a bit of restoration work, could easily be compared to UNESCO World Heritage Sites such as Hoi An in Vietnam and Luang Prabang in Laos. Life is laid-back in Kampot and the town has become an expat retreat with Phnom Penh-ites ducking down here for the fresh air and cooler climate.

Bokor Mountain National Park

① 42 km (90 mins) from Kampot, US$5. Park rangers can speak some English and have a small display board on the flora and fauna in the park at their office. There are dorms (US$5) and double rooms (US$20) and a few basic dishes available. A moto and driver for the day will cost around US$15 or a car around US$30. The new road to Bokor is now open to visitors. The fate of the ruined French casino is unknown and there are still rumours it will be demolished **Bokor Mountain National Park's** plateau, at 1040 m, peers out from the southernmost end of the Elephant Mountains with a commanding view over the Gulf of Thailand and east to Vietnam. Bokor Hill (Phnom Bokor) is densely forested and in the remote and largely untouched woods scientists have discovered 30 species of plant unique to the area. Not for nothing are these called the Elephant Mountains and besides the Asian elephant there are tigers, leopards, wild cows, civets, pigs, gibbons and numerous bird species. At the peak of the mountain is Bokor Hill Station, where eerie, abandoned, moss-covered buildings sit in dense fog. The buildings were built by the French, who attracted by Bokor's relative coolness, established a 'station climatique' on the mountain in the 1920s. In 1970 Lon Nol shut it down and Bokor was quickly taken over by Communist guerrillas; it later became a strategic military base for the Khmer Rouge. In more recent years there was a lot of guerrilla activity in the hills, but the area is now safe, with the exception of the danger, ever-present in Cambodia, of landmines. The ruins are surprisingly well preserved but bear evidence of their tormented past. There is a double waterfall called Popokvil Falls, a 2-km walk from the station, which involves wading through a stream, though in the wet season this is nigh on impossible.

Kbal Romeas caves and temple
Ten kilometres outside Kampot, on the roads to both Phnom Penh and to Kep, limestone peaks harbour interesting caves with stalactites and pools. It is here that you can find one of Cambodia's hidden treasures – an 11th-century temple slowly being enveloped by stalactites and hidden away in a cave in Phnom Chhnok, next to the village of Kbal Romeas. The temple, which is protected by three friendly monks, was discovered by Adhemer Leclere in 1866. Many motos (US$3-4) and cars (US$10) now do trips.

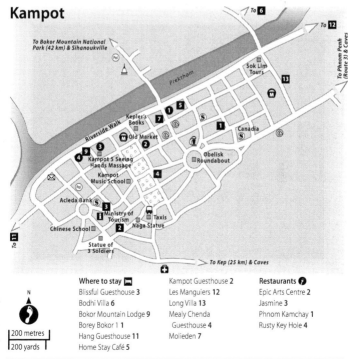

Kampot

To **6**

To **12**

To Bokor Mountain National Park (42 km) & Sihanoukville

To Phnom Penh (Route 3) & Caves

Prekthom

Sok Lim Tours

13

Kepler's Books

7

5

Riverside Walk

Old Market

2

1

Canadia

3

9

4

Kampot 5 Seeing Hands Massage

Obelisk Roundabout

Kampot Music School

4

Acleda Bank

3

Ministry of Tourism

Taxis

Naga Statue

Chinese School

2

Statue of 3 Soldiers

To Kep (25 km) & Caves

N

Where to stay 🛏	Kampot Guesthouse **2**	**Restaurants** 🍴
Blissful Guesthouse **3**	Les Manguiers **12**	Epic Arts Centre **2**
Bodhi Villa **6**	Long Villa **13**	Jasmine **3**
Bokor Mountain Lodge **9**	Mealy Chenda	Phnom Kamchay **1**
Borey Bokor 1 **1**	Guesthouse **4**	Rusty Key Hole **4**
Hang Guesthouse **11**	Molieden **7**	
Home Stay Café **5**		

200 metres
200 yards

ⓘ *From Jul to Oct Kep is subject to the southeast monsoon, occasionally rendering the beach dangerous for swimming because of the debris brought in.*

Tucked in on the edge of the South China Sea, Kep was established in 1908 by the French as a health station for their government officials and families. The ruins of their holiday villas stand along the beachfront and in the surrounding hills. They were largely destroyed during the civil war under Lon Nol and by the Khmer Rouge and were then further ransacked during the famine of the early 1980s when starving Cambodians raided the villas for valuables to exchange for food.

At the time of publication, Kep still hadn't hit the radar of many international tourists. It is very popular on weekends with holidaying Cambodians who have managed to keep this idyllic town one of the country's best-kept secrets. Beautiful gardens and lush green landscape juxtaposed against the blue waters make it one of the most wonderfully relaxing places in the country. The town itself only has one major beach, a pebbly murky water pool that doesn't really compare with Sihanoukville beaches but they can be found at almost all of the 13 outlying islands where you can snorkel and dive although this is better around the islands off Sihanoukville; Kep is considerably more beautiful than Sihanoukville and much more relaxing. It is famous for the freshly caught crab that is best eaten on the beach (US$1.50 per kilo) and the *tik tanaout jiu*, palm wine. From Kep it is possible to hire a boat to **Rabbit Island** (Koh Toensay). Expect to pay about US$10 to hire a boat for the day. There are four half-moon beaches on this island which have finer, whiter sand than Kep beach.

Southern Cambodia listings

For hotel and restaurant price codes and other relevant information, see pages 8-9.

☺ Where to stay

Sihanoukville *p37, map p38*
Places on the relatively undeveloped Otres Beach may appear and disappear relatively quickly. Check in town with other travellers to see what is open there.

$$$$ The Independence Boutique Resort and Spa, Independence Beach, T034-934300, www.independencehotel.net. The most gorgeous hotel in town, beautifully restored to all its modernist glory. The rooms are minimalist, chic and complete with a/c, TV, bath and other luxuries. Great sea views from the hilltop perch, it's also set in some pleasing gardens with a pool. This is exactly the kind of thing Sihanoukville needs to pull itself out of its current malaise. You can also haggle the rates down when it is quiet. Highly recommended.

$$$$-$$$ Sokha Beach Resort and Spa, St 2 Thnou, Sangkat 4, Sokha Beach, T034-935999, www.sokhahotels.com. A de luxe, 180-room beachfront resort and spa, set amid an expansive 15 ha of beachfront gardens and fronting a pristine white sandy beach. Guests have a choice between hotel suites or private bungalows dotted in the tropical gardens. The hotel has fantastic facilities including a landscaped pool, tennis court, archery range, children's club and in-house Filipino band at night. Rooms are impressive. The hotel has very low occupancy, so check if it can offer a discount as it's always running special deals.

$$$-$ Beach Road Hotel, Serendipity Rd, T012-995175, www.beachroad-hotel.com. Excellent value, well-run and maintained hotel with a large range of rooms to fit most budgets; prices drop during low season. All rooms are en suite, with TV, a/c, free Wi-Fi and hot water. The clincher is the gorgeous pool. There's a reasonable and decent bar attached.

\$\$ Chez Claude, between Sokha Beach and Independence Beach, T034-934100. A beautiful hillside spot with 9 bungalows representing a cross-section of indigenous housing. The restaurant has fantastic views.

\$\$ Reef Resort, Serendipity Beach, T012-315338, www.reefresort.com.kh. Well run, small hotel at the top of the hill near the garish golden lions roundabout. Rooms are a touch overpriced but there is a nice pool and breakfast included. Bar and restaurant. Probably the best mid-range place in town. Book ahead. Recommended.

\$\$-\$ Chez Mari-yan, Sankat 3, Khan Mittapheap, T034-933709. Currently the best bungalow-style place to stay in this end of town. Offers a block of hotel rooms and simple wooden and concrete bungalows perched on stilts at the top of a hill affording nice sea views. Restaurant sports a short menu that features fish, squid and crab.

\$\$-\$ Orchidée Guesthouse, Tola St, T034-933639, www.orchidee-guesthouse.com. Well run, clean and well-aired rooms, with a/c and hot water. Restaurant with Khmer and Western seafood. Nice pool area, a 5-min walk to the Ochheauteal Beach.

\$ Castaways, Otres Beach. Friendly place with basic bungalows and rooms directly on the beach. All are en suite and have fans. Good electricity supply that should be 24 hrs in high season.

\$ G'Day Mate, Ekareach St, T012-280947. Decent enough rooms, fan and a/c, all with TV and fridge. They run a good bar and restaurant and also a (sporadic) bus service to Kampot and Kep.

\$ Mealy Chenda, on the crest of Weather Station Hill, T012-419219. Very popular hotel offering accommodation to suit a wide range of budgets from dorm rooms through to a/c double rooms. Sparkly clean with fantastic views from the restaurant.

\$ Motel 7, Ochheuteal Beach, T015-207719. Set just back from the beach on the road, this is a new, stylish and simple guesthouse. All rooms have en suite facilities, cable TV and free Wi-Fi; the pricier ones also have a/c and hot water. Friendly owners were planning to set up a small coffee and ice cream parlour.

\$ Ocean Front, Otres Beach, T012-478531. Reasonably well-run place with the glass fronted rooms laid-out looking onto the beach. The rooms are a bit dingy though. Claims to have electricity all day in high season. Every room has fan and cold water en suite bathrooms.

\$ Sakal Bungalows, near the end of Weather Station Hill, T012-806155, www.sakalbungalows.com. A mix of fan and a/c rooms and bungalows available in this spotless and well-run mini-resort. Restaurant, bar and cheap internet also available. Closest bungalows to Victory Beach. Popular and cheap.

\$ Utopia, Serendipity Rd, T034-934319, www.utopiacambodia.com. It's hard to figure out if this is a new concept in budget travel – the bunks in the dorm rooms are completely free (they also have private rooms for US\$5) – or if it's the beginning of some kind of Beach-like cult. The avowed aim here is partying with poolside raves and an endless supply of fries and burgers. There's nothing remotely Khmer about the experience on offer here but it might indicate one possible future for budget travel.

Sihanoukville islands

\$\$ Lazy Beach, Koh Rung Samloem, booking office is just past **Seahorse Bungalows**, T016-214211, www.lazybeachcambodia.com. Simple, clean bungalows set by a stunning beach. They charge US\$10 per person per single boat transfer to reach the island. Serve up a good array of food as well.

\$ Koh Ru, Koh Russie Island, booking office just past **Sea Horse Bungalows**, T012-366660. This is a quaint collection of simple fan bungalows and dorm rooms in a lovely beachside location. Totally relaxed and quiet, this is a decent spot to really get away from it all. Also serves food and drinks. Boat transfers US\$10.

Koh Kong and around *p39*

With the road to Phnom Penh and Sihanoukville now completed, accommodation and other facilities in Koh Kong are improving.

$$-$ Apex Koh Kong, Street 8, T016-307919, www.apexkohkong.com. With a pool, free Wi-Fi, friendly staff and good food this is easily one of the best places to stay in Koh Kong. The bright, fresh rooms, all set around a courtyard, have cable TV, hot water and a/c. Excellent value. Recommended.

$$-$ Asean Hotel, riverfront, T012-936667. Good rooms with a/c, bathtubs, cable TV. The ones at the front have balconies and river views. There's a decent internet café downstairs. Friendly owners and well run. Recommended.

$$-$ Koh Kong City Hotel, riverfront, T035-936777, kkcthotel.netkhmer.com. This biggish hotel by the river has decent, clean rooms, the best of which have great river views. Staff are a little indifferent but it makes for a good place to stay. Rooms are a/c with cable TV and hot-water en suite facilities throughout.

Kampot and around *p42, map p43*

There's a good range of accommodation.

$$$-$$ Bokor Mountain Lodge, T033-932314, www.bokorlodge.com. Old colonial property on the river front that has had several incarnations and was once even an HQ for the Khmer Rouge. It has bags of atmosphere and is probably the best spot in town for an icy sundowner. All rooms en suite with a/c, cable TV.

$$$-$$ Les Manguiers, 2 km north of town, T092-330050, www.mangokampot.com. Cute little French-run guesthouse. Set by the river amidst paddies and swaying tropical trees this is a relaxing place to spend a couple of days. Good bungalows with fans or a/c; some rooms also in main building. Offers free bicycles to guests.

$$-$ Borey Bokor Hotel 1, T092-978168, boreybokorhotel@yahoo.com. In an ostentatious style with all rooms offering a/c, fridge and comfy beds.

$$-$ Home Stay Café, T077-526443, www.homestaycafe.com. Basic, clean rooms, fan and bathroom. Restaurant offering panoramic views of Mount Bokor.

$ Blissful Guesthouse, next to Acleda Bank, T092-494331, www.blissfulguesthouse.com. Converted colonial building with lovely surrounding gardens. Rooms are simple with mosquito net, fan and attached bath. High on atmosphere and very popular with locals and expats. Recommended.

$ Bodhi Villa, 2 km northwest of town on Teuk Chhou Rd, T012-728884, www.bodhivilla.com. Cheap, friendly, well-run and popular budget guesthouse in a good location just outside town, set on the river bank. Owners seem well-intentioned, linking into local volunteer projects, though some might consider that the hedonistic atmosphere and roaring speedboat which they've introduced to the peaceful river detracts from their efforts. Basic rooms, simple bungalows and US$1 a night dorm.

$ Long Villa, T092-251418, T012-731400. Very friendly, well-run guesthouse. The unspectacular though functional rooms vary from en suite with a/c and TV through to fan with shared facilities. Recommended.

$ Molieden, a block from the main bridge, T012-820779, chuy_seth@yahoo.com. A surprisingly good find, its hideous facade gives way to a very pleasant interior. Large, tastefully decorated modern art deco rooms with TV and fan. The rooftop restaurant also serves some of the best Western food in town. Very good value with free Wi-Fi.

Bokor Mountain National Park *p42*

The park rangers run a simple guesthouse at the hill station – youth-hostel style. There are bunk beds (US$5) and doubles (US$20), with clean shared toilets and showers. Bring your own food: there is a large kitchen available for guests. Pack warm clothes and waterproofs.

Kep *p44*

Accommodation in Kep is better and cheaper than in the rest of the country.

$$$$ Knai Bang Chatt, T078-888556, www.knaibangchatt.com. Set in a restored 20th-century modernist villa, this property seeks to recreate an elitist and colonial atmosphere. Some people will love the banality of exclusivity – others may judge that their money would be better spent elsewhere. Rooms come with all the usual luxury amenities.

$$$-$$ The Vana Guesthouse, T012-755038, www.vannabungalows.com. On the hill before Le Bout Du Monde, this guesthouse comprises 4 attractive thatch-roofed bungalows with attached bathrooms and Western toilet. They are clean but simple with double beds, mosquito nets and little more. The open, thatched restaurant and terrace has a friendly and sedate atmosphere and the food is also good. Staff are friendly and more than willing to organize boat trips to the offshore islands.

$$$-$ Veranda Resort and Bungalows, next door to N4, further up Kep Mountain, T033-399035, www.veranda-resort.com. Superb accommodation. Large wooden bungalows, each with a good-sized balcony, fan, mosquito net and nicely decorated mosaic bathroom. The more expensive of these include very romantic open-air beds. The restaurant offers the perfect vista of the ocean and surrounding countryside. Epicureans will love the variety of international cuisines including poutine of Quebec, smoked ham linguini, fish fillet with olive sauce (all under US$3). Recommended.

$$ The Beach House, T012-712750, www.thebeachhousekep.com. Arguably the nicest spot to stay in Kep. Great rooms, nearly all of which look out onto the mesmeric ocean; all have a/c, hot water, TV. They have a small pool and soothing chill-out area. Unpretentious and good value. The staff can sometimes appear to be half-asleep but are very friendly when provoked. Recommended.

🍴 Restaurants

Sihanoukville *p37, map p38*

$$$ Chez Mari-yan, Victory Beach area. Has a good seafood restaurant with probably the nicest setting in Sihanoukville.

$$$-$$ Le Vivier de la La Paillote, top of Weather Station Hill. This is the finest dining establishment in town and one of the best in the country. The service can't be surpassed and it is high on atmosphere.

$$ Holy Cow, Ekareach St, on the way out of town. Ambient restaurant offering a selection of healthy, Western meals – pasta, salads, baked potatoes. The English owner is a long-term resident and very good source of local information. To his credit he has created a lovely atmosphere and provides impeccable working conditions for his staff.

$$ Mick and Craig's, Ochheauteal Beach. Thankfully, the menu here is a lot more creative than the venue's name. Sufficiently large meals with a bit of pizzazz – pizzas, burgers, hummus, etc. The restaurant also offers 'themed food nights', Sun roast, barbecue and 'all you can eat' nights.

$$ Starfish Café, behind Samudera Super market, T034-952011. Small café-cum-bakery in a very peaceful garden setting. Here you can eat great food, while knowing that you are supporting a good cause. The organization was originally established to help rehabilitate people with disabilities and has extended its services to cover a range of poverty-reducing schemes. A very positive place that oozes goodness in its food, environment and service – good Western breakfasts, cakes, sandwiches, salads and coffees. A non-profit massage business has also opened on premises.

$$-$ Cabbage Garden, T011-940171, down a back lane between Golden Lions and town centre; see map, page 38. Open 1000-2300. This restaurant is rightly famous with both locals and resident expats for its incredible Khmer food. The spicy shrimp mango salad is essential. It's a little tricky to find but a real discovery when you do. Highly recommended.

$$-$ Cantina del Mar, Otres Beach, owned by the same people who run the restaurant of the same name in Phnom Penh. You should find authentic Mexican food and cold Mexican beer here.

Koh Kong and around *p39*
There are several places around town that sell Thai food – most of the Khmer-owned hotels listed in Where to stay, above, also serve food or have a restaurant attached. The market is also a good place to pick up fruit and street food.

$$$ Dug Out. Great Western breakfasts. Also serve other meals but it's at its best first thing.

$$$-$ Café Laurent, next to Koh Kong City Hotel, T011-590168. Mon-Sat 0700-0000. This new bistro serves excellent breakfasts, pastas and pizzas. The coffee and bread are also superb and the pastries are not bad either. Highly recommended.

$$-$ Aqua Sunset Bar and Restaurant, riverfront, T035-6378626. Open 0700-2400. Average Thai, Western and Khmer food served here. They also plan to run river sunset cruises every day at 1700. It's still a great spot to sip a sundowner even if the boat is not running.

Kampot and around *p42, map p43*
$$$ Moliended Restaurant, see Where to stay. On the roof of the guesthouse. Extensive selection of pastas, spaghetti, soup and Italian seafood dishes. Fantastic food. Recommended.

$$ Bokor Mountain Lodge, see Where to stay. Great sandwiches made with the best ingredients – the fish and chicken *amok* is also divine. Recommended.

$$ Jasmine, is a riverside eatery set up by a Khmer woman (Jasmine) and her American photographer partner. They offer a slightly more up-market experience than many of the other places along the riverfront, Khmer and Western dishes. Recommended.

$$ Rusty Key Hole Bar and Restaurant, River Rd, past **Bamboo Light**. Run by

the very down-to-earth Mancunian, Christian, **Rusty's** is now something of a local legend. Western food served. Friendly andthe best place to watch football in town. The barbecue seafood and ribs come highly recommended.

$$-$ Home Stay Café. This is an attractive and relaxed bar and restaurant on the riverfront. The rooftop bar is the place to be for spectacular sunsets over the Elephant Mountains.

$ Epic Arts Café. A brilliant little NGO-run establishment in the centre of Kampot. Set up as a project to employ local disabled people, they produce delicious cakes.

Kep *p44*
There are scores of seafood stalls on the beach, just before the tourist centre, that specialize in cooking freshly caught crab. At the tourist office itself there is also a row of restaurants serving crab, shrimp and fish. Nearly every hotel or guesthouse serves food – see also Where to stay entries.

$$-$ The Riel, T017-902771, www.kep-riel-bar.com.This is now Kep's only proper restaurant-cum-café-cum bar. Great friendly atmosphere and decent food should make this establishment a winner. Good rock 'n' roll stories from the owner as well.

🎵 Bars and clubs

Sihanoukville *p37, map p38*
Most resorts, guesthouses and hotels are also home to some kind of bar. In the Serendipity/Ochheuteal beach area, 2 of the most infamous night time hangouts are **Monkey Republic** and **Utopia**. For a Khmer alternative head to one of the Khmer restaurants near the Golden Lions where you will very likely be serenaded by Khmer singers.
Airport, Victory Beach. Set up by the same Russians who own **Snake House** this massive nightclub is located inside a fake aircraft hangar which is home to an actual, real aircraft. Decent beachside spot and free

entry make this place doubly popular when Sihanoukville is busy.

⚙ What to do

Sihanoukville *p37, map p38*
Diving
Scuba Nation Diving Centre, Weather Station Hill, T012-604680, www.dive cambodia.com. This company has the best reputation in the town and is the longest-established PADI dive centre. Prices vary depending on what you want. An Open Water course is US$350, dive tripsare US$70.

Fishing
Tradewinds Charters at The Fishermen's Den Sports Bar, T01-270 2478, a couple of blocks opposite from the Marlin Hotel on Ekareach St, runs daily fishing trips. If you have caught something worth eating, the proprietor, Brian, will organize the restaurant to prepare a lovely meal from the catch.

Massage
Seeing Hands Massage, next to Q&A Book Café on Ekareach St. Open 0900-2100. US$6 per hour. Have a soothing Japanese-style shiatsu massage from the trained blind masseurs.

Koh Kong and around *p39*
Diving and tours
Koh Kong Divers, 243 Riverfront Rd. T035-690 0073, www.kohkongdivers.com. The only dive shop in Koh Kong is a professional and well-run operation offering the usual PADI courses, diving and snorkelling trips. They also offer several day trips to local islands, 4WD vehicle sojourns into the nearby Cardamom Mountains and numerous other boat excursions up river to waterfalls and into mangroves. Recommended.

Kampot *p42, map p43*
Massage
There are a couple of great blind masseuse places in town, the best being the **Kampot 5 Seeing Hands**, just back from the river near the Bokor Mountain Lodge. The people here are incredibly warm and friendly and at US$4 per hr, it's a great way to relax.

Tour operators **Cheang Try** is a local Khmer who runs both a motorcycle rental outlet in the centre of Kampot town (T012-974698) and also does guided tours. At 17 Mr Try's entire family was murdered by the Khmer Rouge and he was forced to live alone in the jungle on Elephant Mountain, near Bokor for 18 months. He then returned to fight the Khmer Rouge. If you take a tour with Mr Try to Bokor his experiences really bring the place alive – rather than getting some wooden tourist tour you'll come away with some redolent and powerful memories. Highly recommended.

⊖ Transport

Sihanoukville *p37, map p38*
Bus
All buses depart from the main bus station near the new market unless otherwise stated. Many guesthouses and local tour operators may also offer minibus services but these vary in price and scheduling according to season. Around Khmer New Year and during the peak season you will need to book tickets the day before travel. **Phnom Penh Sorya** and **Paramount** both run several services between 0700 and 1400, US$4 to US$5; **Mekong Express** at 0745, 1430, US$7. Route 4 is quick and comfortable and the trip takes about 4 hrs.

Bus services to **Koh Kong** are developing but there are roughly 2 morning departures a day, 4 hrs, US$13. The Thai border is open until 2000 and buses depart until 2330 from Trat to Bangkok.

Minibuses to/from **Kampot** are presently run on a somewhat ad hoc basis by the G'Day Mate guesthouse (see Where to stay, page 45) US$7.50, 0830 departure and the **Peppercorn Express** (T017-921990), 0830, US$7.50. Both will also pick you up from your guesthouse and need to be booked in advance. **Virak-Buntham** bus company has recently started a Sihanoukville to **Kampot/Kep** service at 0745 from the main bus station.

Taxi

Seats in shared taxis are available to **Phnom Penh** (US$7), **Koh Kong** (US$9) and **Kampot** (US$5). All depart from the taxi stand near the bus station. Private taxis are available and according to the quality of the car vary: Phnom Penh (US$35-US$50), Koh Kong (US$60) and Kampot (US$20-US$25).

Koh Kong and around *p39*
Boat

At time of publication the boat service between Koh Kong and Sihanoukville was suspended and unlikely to be reinstated.

Bus

Bus tickets are available from most main guesthouse and hotels with buses departing from bus station 1 km out of town down Street 3. There are presently about 2-3 departures a day to/from **Sihanoukville** (US$6-10, 4 hrs) and **Phnom Penh** (US$8-US$10, 5 hrs). There are also numerous minibus services to destinations in **Thailand** including Trat, Pattaya and Bangkok, but almost all require a change of bus at the border.

Taxi

To **Sihanoukville**, 4 hrs, leaves from market, US$10 person in share d taxi (6 per car), from 0600 onwards, leaves when full. Private taxi, US$60

Kampot and around *p42, map p43*
Bus

There are 2 buses in both directions run by the **Phnom Penh Sorya Transport Co** between Kampot and **Phnom Penh**. These services also stop in **Kep**. They depart the bus station on Blvd Charles de Gaulle near the central market in Phnom Penh at 0730 and 1315, returning at 0730 and 1230 from Kampot bus stand, US$4.

For buses to/from Sihanoukville see Sihanoukville bus listings, page 49.

Taxi

From **Phnom Penh**, 3 hrs to Kampot. Leaving from Doeum Kor Market on Mao Tse Tung Blvd and not the central market in Phnom Penh, US$3-4, 3 hrs. To **Phnom Penh**, vehicles leave from the truck station next to the **Total** gas station at 0700-1400, US$3.50, private taxi US$35-40. To **Sihanoukville**, US$4, private US$20-25, 2 hrs. To **Kep**, US$8, return US$14-15.

Kep *p44*

Kep is only 25 km from Kampot. The road is good and the journey can be made in 30-45 mins. A large white horse statue marks the turn-off to Kep. Buses now run twice a day between Kep/Kampot and Phnom Penh (see above).

🛈 Directory

Sihanoukville *p37, map p38*
Banks 4 banks in town (often shut): Acleda, UCB, Canadia and the Mekong Bank, all on Ekareach St. UCB and Canadia offer Visa/MasterCard cash advances. Cash advances at Samudera Supermarket. Lucky Web, on Weather Station Hill, charges 4% commission. **Internet** Several places around town, particularly near beaches. 3000-8000 riel per hr.

Kampot and around *p42, map p43*
Banks Canadia Bank, close to the Borey Bokor 1 Hotel. Cash advances on Visa and MasterCard. **Internet** On the road between the river and central roundabout, US$1 per hr. International calls around 600-900 riel per min.

Northeast Cambodia

A wild and rugged landscape, consisting of the three provinces of Ratanakiri, Mondulkiri and Stung Treng, greets any visitor to Cambodia's remote northeast region. Vast forested swathes of sparsely inhabited terrain spread north and eastwards toward Vietnam and Laos and are home to several distinct ethnic groups. The thick jungles also provide sanctuary to the majority of Cambodia's few remaining tigers.

During the civil war, the Northeast was cut off from the rest of the country. Then came years of bad transport links, with only the most committed making the arduous run up from up Phnom Penh. Yet the Northeast, much like the rest of the country, is now developing. A new Chinese-built road, including a road bridge over the river in Stung Treng, forms a strong link between Cambodia and Laos, cutting hours off the journey time.

Framing its western edge, and cutting it off from the rest of the country, is the Mekong River. It bifurcates, meanders and braids its way through the country and represents in its width a yawning chasm and watery superhighway that connects the region with Phnom Penh. Stung Treng and Kratie are located on this mighty river and despite the lack of any kind of riverboat service are still excellent places to view the elusive Irrawaddy River Dolphin.

The dust-blown and wild frontier town of Ban Lung, the capital of Ratanakiri, is slowly emerging as a centre of trekking and adventure travel.

Kompong Cham, Kratie and Stung Treng make up the Mekong Provinces. Despite the Mekong River, its waterway and perpetual irrigation, these provinces are surprisingly economically unimportant and laid back. But with the new Chinese-built road now open and fully functioning – it's easily one of the best in the country – the Northeast's provincial charms may soon be eradicated.

Kompong Cham and around

Kompong Cham is the fourth largest town in Cambodia and is a town of some commercial prosperity owing to its thriving river port and also, it is said, as a result of preferential treatment received from local boy made good, the Prime Minister, Hun Sen. Town and province have a combined population of more than 1.5 million people.

There is nothing in or around Kompong Cham to detain the visitor for long, most merely pass through, en route for Stung Treng and the northeast, but it is a pleasant enough town to rest awhile.

The small town of **Chhlong**, between Kompong Cham and Kratie, is one of Cambodia's best-kept secrets. The small town, nestled on the banks of the Mekong, 41 km from Kratie and 82 km from Kompong Cham, is one of the few places that survived the Khmer Rouge's ransacking and contains a multitude of French colonial buildings and traditional wooden Khmer houses. Of particular interest are the foundations of 120 antique houses and a 19th-century wooden Khmer house supported by 100 columns. Formerly a base for workers to surrounding rubber plantations, it is easy to feel nostalgic for a bygone era in Chhlong, with its wats and monasteries, an old school and charming market set in a colonial-style building. There's a couple of basic guesthouses on the riverfront road should you want to stop here for a night or two: **Penh Chet ($)**, T012-690354, with simple clean rooms and **Mekong Guesthouse ($)**, T012-203896, which is a lovely old atmospheric wooden house, though rooms are a bit dirty. There's also a small market with a few stalls selling noodle and rice dishes. A new road linking Kompong Cham and Kratie, and passing just outside Chhlong, has been built. This shaves about 90 minutes off the original journey time and may place Chhlong on a new travellers' route.

Kratie

Kratie (pronounced 'Kratcheay') is a port town on the Mekong roughly half way between Phnom Penh and Laos. In many ways it is a delightful place with a relaxed atmosphere and some good examples of shophouse architecture, but there is a discernible nefarious undercurrent due to Kratie's reputation as a centre of organized crime and corruption. Yet with the murky majesty of the Mekong dominating the town, sunset is a real highlight in Kratie, as the burning red sun descends slowly below the shore line.

Koh Trong Island, directly opposite Kratie town, has a lovely 8-km stretch of sandy dunes (in the dry season) where you can swim and relax. Aside from the beach, the island consists of small market farms and a simple, laid-back rural life – highly recommended for those who want to chill out. On the south side is a small Vietnamese floating village.

Kratie's main claim to some modicum of fame are the **Irrawaddy dolphins** that inhabit this portion of the Mekong (Kampi pool), 15 km north of the town on the road to Stung Treng. The best time to glimpse these rare and timid creatures is at sunrise or sunset when they are feeding. Motos from the town are US$4-US$5 return, boats then cost US$9 per person or US$7 per person if there is three or more.

Kampi Rapids ① *3 km north of Kampi Dolphin Pool, also known as Kampi resort, 1000 riel*, provides a refreshing and picturesque area to take a dip in the clear Mekong waters (during the dry season). A bridge leads down to a series of scenic thatched huts which provide shelter for the swimmers.

Twenty one kilometres further north of the Kampi pool is **Sambor**, a pre-Angkorian settlement, but today, unfortunately, not a single trace of this ancient heritage exists. The highpoint of a trip to Sambor is more in the getting there, as you pass through beautiful countryside, than in the temples themselves. Replacing the ancient ruins are two temples. The first and most impressive is the 100-column pagoda, rumoured to be the largest new pagoda in the country. It is a replica of the 100-column wooden original, which was built in 1529. During the war, Pol Pot based himself out of the complex, killing hundreds of people and destroying the old pagoda. The new one was built in 1985 (perhaps the builders were slightly overzealous – it features 116 columns). Some 300 m behind the gigantic pagoda sits a much smaller and arguably more interesting temple. The wat still contains many of its original features including a number of wooden pylons that date back 537 years.

Stung Treng
Yet another eponymous provincial capital set at the point where the Sekong River cuts away from the Mekong, Stung Treng is just 40 km from Laos and a stopping-off place on the overland route to Ratanakiri. The town still maintains a wild frontier feel despite losing much of its edge due to the building of the mammoth Chinese road and a striking bridge that has created good links to Laos (see Transport, page 58, for more details on how to reach Laos). Pigs, cows and the odd ox-cart still wander through the town's busy streets but there isn't a lot for tourists around Stung Treng. Tour guides can organize boat runs to a local river dolphin project, cycling trips along the river banks and excursions to some waterfalls making it a friendlier alternative to Kratie. **Lbak Khone**, the 26 km rocky area that the Mekong rapids flow through en route to the Laos border, is one of the country's most stunning areas.

Ratanakiri Province → *For listings, see pages 55-59.*

Ratanakiri is like another planet compared to the rest of Cambodia – dusty, red roads curl through the landscape in summer, while in the rainy season the area becomes lush and green turning the roads into slippery mush. Adventure enthusiasts won't be disappointed, with waterfalls to discover, ethnic minorities to meet, elephants to ride, river trips to take and the beautiful Yaek Lom volcanic lake to take a dip in. Be warned: get there soon as a major new road linking Ban Lung to the outside world is now under construction. Once this has been completed Ban Lung is likely to obscure into just another provincial town.

Ban Lung and around
Ban Lung has been the dusty provincial capital of Ratanakiri Province ever since the previous capital Lumphat was flattened by US bombers trying to 'destroy' the footpaths and tracks that made up the Ho Chi Minh Trail. The dirt tracks that used to suffocate the town with their dry season dust and wet season mud have now been mostly paved, making a visit here more amenable. The town is situated on a plateau dotted with lakes and hills, many of great beauty, and serves as a base from which visitors can explore the surrounding countryside. With the Vietnamese in the east building a road from the nearby Le Thanh/O Yadao border crossing, plans to pave the existing roads into and out

of Ban Lung, and a burgeoning tourist market, mark this part of Cambodia for dramatic change. At present you'll find basic guesthouse accommodation, and food and drink can be obtained in town.

Arriving in Ban Lung Ban Lung is 13 hours from Phnom Penh. It is better to break your journey in Kratie and Stung Treng and take a pickup/taxi from there. The chief mode of transport is the motorbike, which comes with a driver, or not, as required (usually US$5 without driver and US$15 with, but you'll have to haggle). Bus services are sporadic. Cars with driver can be hired for US$40-50 a day.

Places around Ban Lung The name Ratanakiri means 'jewel mountains' in Pali, and presumably comes from the wealth of gems in the hills, but it could just as easily refer to the beauty of the landscape. **Yaek Lom** ① *US$1 and a parking charge of 500 riel*, is a perfectly circular volcanic lake about 5 km east of town and easily reached by motorbike. The crystalline lake is rimmed by protected forest dominated by giant emergents (dipterocarps and shoreas) soaring high into the sky. It takes about one hour to walk around the lake: in doing so you will find plenty of secluded bathing spots, a couple of small jetties and, given the lack of water in town, it is not surprising that most locals and visitors bathe in the wonderfully clear and cool waters of the lake. There is a small 'museum' of ethnography and a couple of minority stilt houses to be seen.

There are three **waterfalls** ① *2000 riel each*, in close proximity to Ban Lung town. **Kachaang Waterfall** is 6 km away. The 12-m high waterfall flows year round and is surrounded by magnificent, pristine jungle and fresh mist rising from the fall. **Katien Waterfall** is a little oasis 7 km northwest of Ban Lung. Believed to have formed from volcanic lava hundreds of years ago, the 10-m plunging falls are sheltered from the outside world by a little rocky grotto. It is one of the better local falls to swim in as it is very secluded (most people will usually have the area to themselves); the water is completely clean. The best waterfall is arguably **Chaa Ong Falls**, with the 30-m falls plunging into a large pool. Those game enough can have a shower behind the crescent-shaped ledge. To get to the waterfalls, follow Highway 19 out of town and branch off 2 km out on the main road in the first village out of Ban Lung: Chaa Ong Falls are 9 km northwest at the intersection, turn right at the village and head for about 5 km to head to Katien Waterfall (follow the signs), the same road heads to Kachaang Waterfall.

The trip to **Ou'Sean Lair Waterfall**, 35 km from Ban Lung, is a wonderful day excursion offering a fantastic cross-section of what is essentially Ratanakiri's main attractions (without the riverside element). From Ban Lung, fields of wind-bent, spindly rubber trees provide a canopy over the road's rolling hills, a legacy left from the French in the 1960s. Punctuating the mottled natural vista is an equally diverse range of ethnic minority settlements. Tampeun and Kreung villages are dotted along the road and about half way (17 km from Ban Lung), in a lovely valley, is a tiny Cham village. The perfect end to the journey is the seven-tiered **Ou'Sean Lair falls**. The falls were reportedly 'discovered' by a Tampeun villager five years ago, who debated as to whether he should tell the Department of Tourism of their existence. In return for turning over the falls, they were named after him. The falls are most spectacular in the wet season but are still pretty alluring during the dry season.

Northeast Cambodia listings

For hotel and restaurant price codes and other relevant information, see pages 8-9.

⊖ Where to stay

Kompong Cham and around *p52*

$$-$ Leap Viraksar Hotel, big yellow building on right just before bridge on way to Kratie, T042-633 7778. Range of rooms from grim-looking fan rooms through to accommodation replete with a/c, TV and bathtubs. Friendly; mini-mart attached.

$$-$ Monorom 2 VIP Hotel, Mort Tunle St, waterfront, T092-777102, www.monorom viphotel.com. With a perfect Mekong setting this new hotel is easily the best in town. Get a room at the front and you'll have a balcony overlooking the river – each comes with bathtub, hot water, cable TV, tea-making facilities and there's free Wi-Fi/internet for guests on the ground floor. Recommended.

$ Rana, T012-696340. Set in a small village just outside Kampong Cham, this is a well-run and engaging homestay programme run by Kheang and her American husband, Don. Set up more for educational purposes than as a business; you can get a real insight into rural life here. Rates include full-board but accommodation is basic. They offer free moto pickup from Kampong Cham if you book for 2 or more nights. Recommended.

Kratie *p52*

$ Balcony Guesthouse, riverfront road, T016-604036, www.balconyguesthouse.net. There are several airy, clean and basic rooms in this villa overlooking the river. There is, of course, a giant, communal balcony which is a great place to lounge and watch Mekong sunsets. Bar, restaurant and internet as well.

$ Oudom Sambath Hotel, 439 River Rd, T072-971502. Well-run place with a friendly English speaking Chinese-Khmer owner. The rooms are huge, with a/c, TV, hot water, etc. The more expensive rooms have large baths

and regal-looking furniture. The huge rooftop balcony has the best views of the Mekong in town – they have rooms up here as well but these fill quickly. Also has a decent and very cheap restaurant. Recommended.

$ Santepheap Hotel, on the river road, T072-971537. Rooms are adequate in this reasonable hotel. It has a quiet atmosphere and the clean and airy rooms come with attached bathrooms, fridge, fan or a/c.

$ Star Guesthouse, beside the market, T072-971663. This has gained the reputation of being the friendliest guesthouse in town. It is very popular with travellers and its rooms are nicely appointed.

$ You Hong Guesthouse, between the taxi rank and the market, T012-957003. Clean rooms with attached bathroom and fan. US$1 extra gets you cable TV. Friendly, helpful owners. The restaurant is often filled with drunk backpackers.

Stung Treng *p53*

$$-$ Hotel Gold River, riverfront, T012-980678. New 4-storey hotel with splendid river views and the only lift in northeastern Cambodia. Each spotless and comfortable room has a hot-water bathtub, cable TV and a/c; the ones at the front offer the river as backdrop. Friendly service and a bargain given the location. Recommended.

$$-$ Ly Ly Guesthouse, opposite the market, T012-937859. Decent Chinese-style hotel with varying types of rooms – all come with private shower/toilet and cable TV. The ones at the back of the building have balconies and are the best value – you have the option of a/c or fan throughout. Friendly with some English spoken. Recommended.

$$-$ Nature Lodge, a few kilometres north of Stung Treng town, T074-637 7767. Gorgeous location set in a nook of the Mekong River is offset by the tired-looking rooms and bungalows. It's just been taken over by a local community group who hope to help this wonderfully sited resort-type set-up reach its full potential. Check in Stung Treng at the XploreAsia office (see What to do, page 57) for more details.

$$-$ Stung Treng Hotel and Guest House, on main road near the river, T016-888335. Decent enough rooms in a good location – a reasonable second option.

Ban Lung and around *p53*
$$-$ Borann Lodge, 800 m east of market, T012-959363. This huge chalet-style villa set down a Ban Lung side street comes with 6 rooms of varying sizes though each has a/c and fan and en suite bathroom with hot water. The owners and staff are very friendly and Borann feels more like a homestay than a guesthouse. Massive wooden model of Angkor and various over-the-top wooden furniture items add to the character. Affiliated with Yaklom Hill Lodge. Recommended.
$$-$ NorDen House, on road to Yaklom Lake, T012-880327, www.nordenhouse yaklom.com. The nearest accommodation to the Yaklom Lake. You'll find a collection of spotless, well-appointed bungalows here each with a/c, TV and en suite hot-water facilities. There are some attractive gardens, a decent restaurant, free Wi-Fi plus they can arrange bus tickets. Owner also rents out the best motorbikes in town. Swedish and Khmer owners. Recommended.
$$-$ Yaklom Hill Lodge, near Yaklom Lake, 6 km east of Ban Lung, T012-644240, www.yaklom.com. Set in a private forest this rustic ecolodge is a bit out of town. Bungalows have balconies and hammocks and are well decorated with local handicrafts and fabrics. Fan, mosquito net, attached bathroom, shower; power is supplied via generator and solar panels. The friendly owner, Sampon, arranges all manner of tours and treks and is the only operator in the area who uses local ethnic minority peoples as guides. Affiliated with Borann Lodge. The food is a bit ropey but still this place is recommended.

$ Sopheap Guest House, next to the market, T012-958746. Clean rooms come complete with hot water, fan or a/c, cable TV and a noisy and lively central location. Get one with a balcony and you'll have a great view of the market life unfolding below you.
$ Tree Top Eco Lodge, Phum Nol, Laban Seak commune, T011-600381, www.treetop-ecolodge.com. Lovely set of large wooden bungalows overlooking a valley on the edge of town. Interiors are well decorated and each room comes complete with adjacent huge balconies and en suite hot-water bathrooms. There are some good communal areas and verandas, a restaurant/bar and free transfers to the bus station. Recommended.

⊘ Restaurants

Kompong Cham and around *p52*
$$ Ho An Restaurant, Monivong St, T042-941234. Large, Chinese restaurant with a good selection of dishes. Friendly service.
$$-$ Lazy Mekong Daze, on the riverfront. British owner Simon provides alcohol, cakes, fish and chips, and Khmer food from this friendly riverside establishment. He also has a free pool table and you can watch the latest football on his TV.
$ Fresh Coffee, same block as **Monorom 2 VIP Hotel** on riverfront. Open 0700-2100. Small new coffee shop selling burgers, cakes and some Khmer food.
$ Smile Restaurant, same block as **Monorom 2 VIP Hotel** on riverfront. Open 0630-2200. Huge Khmer menu with some Western dishes in this new and excellent NGO-connected eatery that helps orphans and kids with HIV. Free Wi-Fi. Recommended.

Kratie *p52*
There are a number of foodstalls along the river at night serving fruit shakes. The market also sells simple dishes during the day.

$$-$ Balcony Guesthouse (see Where to stay above). Serves up an excellent fried British breakfast and various other Western and Khmer dishes from its huge balcony overlooking the river. Good spot for a drink as well. Recommended.

$$-$ Red Sun Falling, on the river road. Open Mon-Sat. Probably the best restaurant in town, it offers a variety of excellent Western dishes and a few Asian favourites. The full monty breakfast is fantastic. Good cocktails. The very friendly proprietor, Joe, also runs a very good bookshop on the premises. Recommended.

$$-$ Star Guesthouse. See Where to stay, above. A decent enough menu but sometimes the prices (almost US$1 for a squeeze of honey) and quality let the place down. Western food, and the home-made bread is excellent.

Stung Treng p53

$ Prochum Tonle Restaurant, at the Sekong Hotel on the riverfront. Some of the best Khmer food in town at this locally renowned restaurant.

$ Sophakmukal, near the market. Beer garden-style restaurant with very good, cheap Cambodian food, curry, *amok*, soup (all under US$1). Very friendly owner. Recommended.

$ Stung Treng Burger, in a side street near the market. Daily 0630-2100. Very friendly owners, fresh decor and good food make this place one of the best spots in town. Great burgers and pizza supplement excellent Khmer food; decent breakfasts too. Recommended.

Ban Lung and around p53

Food options are now improving in Ban Lung with a greater range of fresh fruit and other produce on sale at the market and various small bakeries offering Khmer-style cakes and breads opening up.

$ A' Dam, on the same road as Borann Lodge and Tree Top Eco Lodge. Open 1100(ish)-2400. It's understandable why A'Dam is a popular with both Ban Lung

locals and expat NGO workers. Great Khmer and Western food is piled high and served cheap by the friendly Khmer owners. Also doubles as a bar. Recommended.

$ Apocalypse Bar (near Borann Lodge). You can get decent coffee and tea plus breakfasts at this small eatery attached to the Dutch Couple tour agency.

$ Ratanak Hotel Restaurant. Quite popular, serves a spectacular barbecue that you cook at your table. Cambodian food US$1-2.

$ Tree Top Eco Lodge, see Where to stay, above. Great location for both dinner and a drink but the food isn't all that it could be. Best setting but you can eat better at other places.

⊙ What to do

Stung Treng p53

XploreAsia, on the riverfront near the Hotel Gold River. They are working in conjunction with various local community projects and offer a variety of tours including river excursions, trips to see the dolphins, and cycling and kayaking tours. You should also be able to find out about other tours at the Riverside Guesthouse (see Where to stay, above).

Ban Lung and around p53

Dutch Couple, on road east of the market, T099-531745, www.ecotourismcambodia.info. This is a small and recently opened eco-tourism outfit offering well-equipped, upmarket and pricey tours to various destinations in northeast Cambodia.

Yaklom Hill Lodge, see Where to stay, above. Offer a variety of tours and other adventures. They use their own local ethnic minority guides.

⊖ Transport

Kompong Cham and around p52
Bus

The town is 120 km northeast of Phnom Penh via the well-surfaced Routes 5, 6 and 7. There are regular connections with **Phnom Penh** by shared taxi and numerous bus companies run regular services. Buses also connect to all points north including **Chhlong**, **Kratie**, **Stung Treng** and **Ban Lung.**

Moto/tuk-tuk/taxi
Local transport is by moto, tuk-tuk or taxi. A moto for a day is between US$6-8 and between 500-1000 riel for short trips. Local tuk-tuk driver and guide Mr Vannat has an excellent reputation and is fluent in French and English, T012-995890. US$20 a day for a boat ride.

Kratie *p52*
Bus
Roughly 4 buses a day run to **Phnom Penh,** US$5/US$8, 4-5 hrs, stopping off at **Kompong Cham** en route. **Stung Treng** is served by regular minibuses 0800-1400, US$6, 2 hrs, and at least 1 daily bus, US$4, 2½ hrs; while there is at least 1 minibus a day to **Ban Lung**, US$12, 6 hrs. Many of these buses depart from the bus stand near the river, but you might want to ask at your accommodation if this has changed. You can also find shared taxis plying routes to all destinations though prices fluctuate according to season, road condition and fuel prices.

Motodop
Local transport by motodop US$1 per hr or US$6-7 per day.

Stung Treng *p53*
Before the bridge opened in 2008, Stung Treng used to be the staging post for travel to Laos with regular boats plying the few kilometres upriver to the border. This situation, however, has now completely changed with most travellers heading south from Pakse in Laos, no longer stopping in Stung Treng, preferring instead to take through buses directly to Kratie and Phnom Penh.

Most hotels (**Sekong**, **Riverside**, etc) can organize tickets. Alternatively, you can go directly to the taxi/bus rank. At present there is at least 1 bus a day to **Pakse**, 4½ hrs, US$6, in Laos and through ticketing to **Vientiane** (change in Pakse) is also available, US$35, should you wish to connect directly to the Laos capital. There are a couple of buses to **Phnom Penh** daily, 9 hrs, US$7.50; and the same bus will stop at **Kratie**, US$5. Plenty of minibuses also ply this route.

Pickups and shared taxis connect regularly with **Phnom Penh** via **Kratie**, and with recent road construction the roads should be OK to travel along (if a little bumpy). Shared taxis to **Phnom Penh** leave at 0600 from the taxi rank near the river, 7 hrs, US$15. To **Ban Lung** at 0700 from the taxi rank and the trip takes 4-5 hrs, US$10.

Ban Lung and around *p53*
Bus
With the route from Kompong Cham to Kratie being both shortened and improved plus the plans to upgrade the road into

Ban Lung, journey times between **Ratanakiri** and **Phnom Penh** (and places en route) could be significantly reduced in the near future.

Regular daily buses to **Stung Treng**, 3 hrs, US$6; **Kratie**, 5-6 hrs, US$7; **Kompong Cham**, 6-8 hrs, US$9, **Siem Reap** (14 hrs, change in Skon, US$16), **Phnom Penh**, 9-11hrs, US$9-US$14; and to the **Vietnamese border**, 2½ hrs, US$10, are all available in a variety of mini and larger buses. Share and private taxis are also available with prices fluctuating depending on season, road conditions and price of fuel; ask at your guesthouse/hotel for price approximations on arrival.

Motorbike
Den Norden guesthouse (see Where to stay, above) has a few top-class 250cc and 400cc dirt bikes for rent, from US$25 to US$50 per day.

Kompong Cham and around *p52*
Banks There are 2 banks in town – Acleda and Canadia Bank. Acleda, 0800-1600, will do Western Union transfers and Canadia will do advances on Visa and MasterCard.
Internet ABC computers, in the centre of town, was the only internet shop operating at the time of writing, US$1 per hr, overseas phone calls.

Kratie *p52*
Banks There is an Acleda Bank half way down St 11. It does not offer advances on Visa or MasterCard but is a subsidiary for Western Union. **Internet** You Hong Guesthouse offer a good, cheap connection. Three Star Internet US$4 per hr. There is another internet café near Phnom Penh Transport bus office but at the time of writing it was US$4 per hr.

Stung Treng *p53*
Banks There are no banks in town.
Internet Available at the computer shop opposite the market and the Sekong Hotel, US$4 per hr. **Telephone** There are telephone shops all over town.

Ban Lung and around *p53*
Banks Amazingly ANZ bank have opened an ATM near the airport. Details are sketchy if foreign bank cards are being accepted by this machine so it's best not to rely on it for a source of cash. The Mountain Guesthouse and the Ratanak Hotel both change TCs but allow at least 3 days for your cheques to clear. **Internet** CIC near Sovannikiri Hotel.
Medical services The hospital is on the road north towards O Chum. Dr Vannara, T012-970359, speaks very good English.
Post office In the centre of town.

Angkor

The huge temple complex of Angkor, the ancient capital of the powerful Khmer Empire, is one of the archaeological treasures of Asia and the spiritual and cultural heart of Cambodia. Angkor Wat is arguably the greatest temple within the complex, both in terms of grandeur and sheer magnitude. After all, it is the biggest religious monument in the world, its outer walls clad with one of the longest continuous bas-relief ever created. The diverse architectural prowess and dexterity of thousands of artisans is testified by around 100 brilliant monuments in the area. Of these the Bayon, with its beaming smiles; Banteay Srei, which features the finest intricate carvings; and the jungle temple of Ta Prohm are unmissable. Others prefer the more understated but equally brilliant temples of Neak Pean, Preah Khan and Pre Rup.

The petite town of Siem Reap sits nearby the Angkor complex, and is home to a gamut of world-class hotels, restaurants and bars. A hop, skip and a jump from the town is Southeast Asia's largest lake, the Tonlé Sap, with floating villages, teeming with riverine life.

Visiting Angkor

Getting there

Air The airport ① *T063-963148*, is 7 km from Siem Reap, the town closest to the Angkor ruins (see Transport, page 83), with flights from Phnom Penh, Ho Chi Minh City, Bangkok and Vientiane. A moto into town is US$1, a taxi US$7. Guesthouse owners often meet flights. Visas can be issued upon arrival US$20 (฿1000), photo required.

Boat From Phnom Penh, US$35, five to six hours. The trip is a good way to see the mighty Tonlé Sap Lake. It is a less appealing option in the dry season when low water levels necessitate transfers to small, shallow draft vessels. In case of extremely low water levels a bus or pickup will need to be taken for part of the trip. The mudbank causeway between the lake and the outskirts of Siem Reap is hard to negotiate and some walking may be necessary (it's 12 km from Bindonville harbour to Siem Reap). Boats depart from the Phnom Penh Port on Sisowath Quay (end of 106 Street) 0700, departing Siem Reap 0700 from Chong Khneas about 12 km away on the Tonlé Sap Lake. Tickets and enquiries, T012-581358 (a motodop will cost US$2 to get here).

Bus The air-conditioned buses are one of the most convenient and comfortable ways to go between Phnom Penh and Siem Reap, US$6-11, six hours. Almost every guesthouse or

Beating the crowds

These days avoiding traffic within the Angkor complex is difficult but still moderately achievable. As it stands, there is a pretty standard one-day tour itinerary that includes: Angkor Wat (sunrise), Angkor Thom, the Bayon, etc (morning), break for lunch, Ta Prohm (afternoon), Preah Khan (afternoon) and Phnom Bakheng (sunset). If you reverse the order, peak hour traffic at major temples is dramatically reduced. As many tour groups troop into Siem Reap for lunch this is an opportune time to catch a peaceful moment in the complex, just bring a packed lunch or eat at 1100 or 1400.

To avoid the masses at the draw-card attraction, Angkor Wat, try to walk around the temple, as opposed to through it. Sunset at Phnom Bakheng has turned into a circus fiasco, so aim for Angkor or the Bayon at this time as they are both quiet in comparison.

Sunrise is still relatively peaceful at Angkor, grab yourself the prime position behind the left-hand pond (you need to depart Siem Reap no later than 0530), though there are other stunning early morning options, such as Srah Srang or Bakong. Bakheng gives a beautiful vista of Angkor in the early-mid morning.

hotel sells tickets although it is easy enough to pick up from the bus stations/terminal. In peak periods, particularly Khmer New Year, it is important to purchase tickets a day or two prior to travel. A shared taxi from Phnom Penh will cost you US$10.

Getting around

Most of the temples within the Angkor complex (except the Roluos Group) are located in an area 8 km north of Siem Reap, with the area extending across a 25 km radius. The Roluos Group are 13 km east of Siem Reap and further away is Banteay Srei (32 km).

Cars with drivers and guides are available from larger hotels from around US$25 toUS$30 per day plus US$25 for a guide. An excellent guiding service by car is provided by **Mr Hak** ① T012-540336, www.angkortaxidriver.com, who offers a variety of packages and tours around Angkor and the surrounding area. The Angkor Tour Guide Association and most other travel agencies can also organize this. Expect to pay around US$10-12 per day for a moto unless the driver speaks good English, in which case the price will be higher. This price will cover trips to the Roluos Group of temples but not to Banteay Srei. No need to add more than a dollar or two to the price for getting to Banteay Srei unless the driver is also a guide and can demonstrate to you that he is genuinely going to show you around. Tuk-tuks and their ilk have appeared in recent years and a trip to the temples on a motorbike-drawn cart is quite a popular option for two people, U$14-17 a day (maximum two people).

Bicycle hire, US$2-3 per day from most guesthouses, represents a nice option for those who feel reasonably familiar with the area. The White Bicycles scheme, set up by Norwegian expats (see Transport, page 83), offers bikes forUS$2 per day withUS$1.50 of that going straight into local charities and no commission to the hotels and is recommended. If you are on a limited schedule and only have a day or two to explore you won't be able to cover an awful lot of the temples on a pedal bike as the searing temperatures and sprawling layout can take even the most advanced cyclists a considerable amount of time. Angkor Wat and Banteay Srei have official parking sites, 1000 riel and at the other temples you can quite safely park and lock your bikes in front of a drink stall. You can also charter a helicopter, see page 82. Elephants are stationed near the Bayon or at the South Gate of

Angkor Thom during the day. In the evenings, they are located at the bottom of Phnom Bakheng, taking tourists up to the summit for sunset. ▸▸ *See What to do, page 82.*

Best time to visit

Angkor's peak season coincides with the dry season, November-February. Not only is this the driest time of year it is also the coolest (which can still be unbearably hot). The monsoon lasts from June to October or November. At this time it can get very muddy.

Tourist information

Guides can be invaluable when navigating the temples, with the majority being able to answer most questions about Angkor as well as providing additional information about Cambodian culture and history. Most hotels and travel agents will be able to point you in the direction of a good guide. The **Khmer Angkor Tour Guide Association** ① *on the road to Angkor, T063-964347, www.khmerangkortourguide.com,* has pretty well-trained guides. Most of the guides here are well briefed and some speak English better than others. The going rate is US$20-25 per day. There is a new **tourist office** ① *at the far end of Sivatha Street (towards the crocodile farm), 0730-1100 and 1430-1700.*

Temple fees and hours   A one-day pass costs US$20, three-day pass US$40, seven-day pass US$60. The seven-day pass is valid for any seven days (they don't have to be consecutive) one month from the purchase date. Most people will be able to cover the majority of the temples within three days. If you buy your ticket after 1715 the day before, you get a free sunset thrown in. The complex is open daily 0530-1830. You will need to pay additional fees if you wish to visit Beng Melea (US$5), Phnom Kulen (US$20) or Koh Ker (US$10); payable at the individual sites.

Safety   Landmines were planted on some outlying paths to prevent Khmer Rouge guerrillas from infiltrating the temples; they have pretty much all been cleared by now, but it is safer to stick to well-used paths. Be wary of snakes in the dry season. The very poisonous Hanuman snake (lurid green) is fairly common in the area.

Photography   A generalization, but somewhat true, is that black and white film tends to produce better-looking tourist pictures than those in colour. The best colour shots usually include some kind of contrast against the temples, a saffron-clad monk or a child. Don't forget to ask if you want to include people in your shots. In general, the best time to photograph the great majority of temples is before 0900 and after 1630.

Itineraries

The temples are scattered over an area in excess of 160 sq km. A half-day would only allow enough time to visit the South Gate of Angkor Thom, Bayon and Angkor Wat. There are three so-called 'circuits'. The **Petit Circuit** takes in the main central temples including Angkor Wat, Bayon, Baphuon and the Terrace of the Elephants. The **Grand Circuit** takes a wider route, including smaller temples like Ta Prohm, East Mebon and Neak Pean. The **Roluos Group Circuit** ventures further afield still, taking in the temples near Roluos – Lolei, Preah Ko and Bakong. Here are some options for visiting Angkor's temples:

One day Angkor Wat (sunrise or sunset), South Gate of Angkor Thom, Angkor Thom Complex (Bayon, Elephant Terrace, Royal Palace) and Ta Prohm. This is a hefty schedule for one day; you'll need to arrive after 1615 and finish just after 1700 the following day.

Two days The same as above but with the inclusion of the rest of the Angkor Thom, Preah Khan, Srah Srang (sunrise), and at a push, Banteay Srei.

Three days Day 1 Sunrise at Angkor Wat; morning South Gate of Angkor Thom, Angkor Thom complex (aside from Bayon); Ta Prohm; late afternoon-sunset at the Bayon. **Day 2** Sunrise Srah Srang; morning Banteay Kdei and Banteay Srei; late afternoon Preah Khan; sunset at Angkor Wat. **Day 3** Sunrise and morning Roluos; afternoon Ta Keo and sunset either at Bakheng or Angkor Wat. Those choosing to stay one or two days longer should try to work Banteay Samre, East Mebon, Neak Pean and Thomannon into their itinerary. A further two to three days warrants a trip to Prasat Kravan, Ta Som, Beng Melea and Kbal Spean.

Background

Khmer Empire

Under Jayavarman VII (1181-1218) the complex stretched more than 25 km east to west and nearly 10 km north to south, approximately the same size as Manhattan. For five centuries (ninth-13th), the court of Angkor held sway over a vast territory. At its height Khmer influence spanned half of Southeast Asia, from Burma to the southernmost tip of Indochina and from the borders of Yunnan to the Malay Peninsula. The only threat to this great empire was a river-borne invasion in 1177, when the Cham used a Chinese navigator to pilot their canoes up the Mekong. Scenes are depicted in bas-reliefs of the Bayon temple.

Jayavarman II (AD 802-835) founded the Angkor Kingdom, then coined Hariharalaya to the north of the Tonlé Sap, in the Roluos region (Angkor), in AD 802. Later he moved the capital to Phnom Kulen, 40 km northeast of Angkor, where he built a Mountain Temple and Rong Shen shrine. After several years he moved the capital back to the Roluos region. **Jayavarman III** (AD 835-877) continued his father's legacy and built a number of shrines at Hariharalaya. Many historians believe he was responsible for the initial construction of the impressive laterite pyramid, Bakong, considered the great precursor to Angkor Wat. Bakong, built to symbolize Mount Meru, was later embellished and developed by Indravarman. **Indravarman** (AD 877-889) overthrew his predecessor violently and undertook a major renovation campaign in the capital Hariharalaya. The majority of what stands in the Roluos Group today is the work of Indravarman. A battle between Indravarman's sons destroyed the palace and the victor and new king **Yasovarman I** (AD 889-900) moved the capital from Roluos and laid the foundations of Angkor itself. He dedicated the temple to his ancestors. His new capital at Angkor was called Yasodharapura, meaning 'glory-bearing city', and here he built 100 wooden ashramas, retreats (all of which have disintegrated today). Yasovarman selected Bakheng as the location for his temple-mountain and after flattening the mountain top, set about creating another Mount Meru. The temple he constructed was considered more complex than anything built beforehand, a five-storey pyramid with 108 shrines. A road was then built to link the former and present capitals of Roluos and Bakheng. Like the Kings before him, Yasovarman was obliged to construct a major waterworks and the construction of the reservoir – the East Baray (now completely dry) – was considered an incredible feat. After Yasovarman's death in AD 900 his son **Harshavarman** (AD 900-923) assumed power for the next 23 years. During his brief

Motifs in Khmer sculpture

Apsaras These are regarded as one of the greatest invention of the Khmers. The gorgeous temptresses – born, according to legend, 'during the churning of the Sea of Milk' – were Angkor's equivalent of pin-up girls and represented the ultimate ideal of feminine beauty. They lived in heaven where their sole raison d'être was to have eternal sex with Khmer heroes and holy men. The apsaras are carved in seductive poses with splendidly ornate jewellery and clothed in the latest Angkor fashion. Different facial features suggest the existence of several races at Angkor. Together with the five towers of Angkor Wat they have become the symbol of Khmer culture. The god-king himself possessed an apsara-like retinue of court dancers – impressive enough for Chinese envoy Chou Ta-kuan to write home about it in 1296.

Garuda Mythical creature – half-man, half-bird – was the vehicle of the Hindu god, Vishnu, and the sworn enemy of the nagas. It appeared relatively late in Khmer architecture.

Kala Jawless monster commanded by the gods to devour his own body – made its first appearance in lintels at Roluos. The monster represented devouring time and was an early import from Java.

Makara Mythical water-monster with a scaly body, eagles' talons and an elephantine trunk.

Naga Sacred snake. These play an important part in Hindu mythology and the Khmers drew on them for architectural inspiration. Possibly more than any other single symbol or motif, the naga is characteristic of Southeast Asia and decorates objects throughout the region. The naga is an aquatic serpent and is intimately associated with water (a key component of Khmer prosperity). In Hindu mythology, the naga coils beneath and supports Vishnu on the cosmic ocean. The snake also swallows the waters of life, these only being set free to reinvigorate the world after Indra ruptures the serpent with a bolt of lightning. Another version has Vishnu's servants pulling at the serpent to squeeze the waters of life from it (the so-called churning of the sea, see box, page 66).

Singha Lion in stylized form; often the guardians to temples.

reign, Harshavarman is believed to have built Baksei Chamkrong (north-east of Phnom Bakheng) and Prasat Kravan (the 'Cardamom Sanctuary'). His brother, **Ishanarvarman II** (AD 923-928), resumed power upon his death but no great architectural feats were recorded in this time. In 928, **Jayavarman IV** moved the capital 65 km away to Koh Ker. Here he built the grand state temple Prasat Thom, an impressive seven-storey, sandstone pyramid. Following the death of Jayavarman, things took a turn for the worst. Chaos ensued under **Harshavarman's II** weak leadership and over the next four years, no monuments were known to be erected. Jayavarman's IV nephew, **Rajendravarman** (AD 944-968), took control of the situation and it's assumed he forcefully relocated the capital back to Angkor. Rather than moving back into the old capital Phnom Bakheng, he marked his own new territory, selecting an area south of the East Baray as his administrative centre. Here, in AD 961 he constructed the state temple, Pre Rup, and constructed the temple, East Mebon (AD 953), in the middle of the baray. Srah Srang, Kutisvara and Bat Chum were also constructed, with the help of his chief architect, Kavindrarimathana. It was towards the end of his reign that he started construction on Banteay Srei, considered one of the finest examples of Angkorian craftsmanship in the country. Rajendravarman's son **Jayavarman V** (AD 968-1001) became the new king in 968. The administrative centre was renamed Jayendranagari and yet again, relocated. More than compensating for the unfinished Ta Keo was Jayavarman's V continued work on Banteay Srei. Under his supervision the splendid temple was completed and dedicated to his father.

Aside from successfully extending the Khmer Empire's territory **King Suryavarman I** (1002-1049), made a significant contribution to Khmer architectural heritage. He presided over the creation of a new administrative centre – the Royal Palace (in Angkor Thom) – and the huge walls that surround it. The next in line was **Udayadityavarman II** (1050-1066), the son of Suryavarman I. The Baphuon temple-mountain was built during his relatively short appointment. After overthrowing his Great-Uncle Dharanindravarman, **SuryavarmanII** (1112-1150), the greatest of Angkor's god-kings, came to power. His rule marked the highest point in Angkorian architecture and civilization. Not only was he victorious in conflict, having beaten the Cham whom couldn't be defeated by China, he was responsible for extending the borders of the Khmer Empire into Myanmar, Malaya and Siam. This aside, he was also considered one of the era's most brilliant creators. Suryavarman II was responsible for the construction of Angkor Wat, the current-day symbol of Cambodia. Beng Melea, Banteay Samre and Thommanon are also thought to be the works of this genius. He has been immortalized in his own creation – in a bas-relief in the South Gallery of Angkor Wat the glorious King Suryavarman II sitting on top of an elephant. After a period of political turmoil, which included the sacking of Angkor, **Jayavarman VII** seized the throne in 1181 and set about rebuilding his fiefdom. He created a new administrative centre – the great city of Angkor Thom. The mid-point of Angkor Thom is marked by his brilliant Mahayana Buddhist state temple, the Bayon. It is said that the Bayon was completed in 21 years. Jayavarman took thousands of peasants from the rice fields to build it, which proved a fatal error, for rice yields decreased and the empire began its decline as resources were drained. The temple, which consists of sculptured faces of Avolokiteshavara (the Buddha of compassion and mercy) are often said to also encompass the face of their great creator, Jayavarman VIII. He was also responsible for restoring the Royal Palace, renovating Srah Srang and constructing the Elephant Terrace, the Terrace of the Leper King and the nearby baray (northeast of Angkor Thom), Jayataka reservoir. At the centre of his reservoir he built Neak Pean. Jayavarman VII adopted Mahayana Buddhism; Buddhist principles replaced the Hindu pantheon, and were invoked as the basis of royal authority. This spread of Buddhism is thought to have caused some of the earlier Hindu temples to be neglected. The king paid tribute to his Buddhist roots through his monastic temples – Ta Prohm and Preah Khan.

The French at Angkor

Thai ascendency and eventual occupation of Angkor in 1431, led to the city's abandonment and the subsequent invasion of the jungle. Four centuries later, in 1860, Henri Mouhot – a French naturalist – stumbled across the forgotten city, its temple towers enmeshed in the forest canopy. Locals told him they were the work of a race of giant gods. Only the stone temples remained; all the wooden secular buildings had decomposed in the intervening centuries. In 1873 French archaeologist Louis Delaporte removed many of Angkor's finest statues for 'the cultural enrichment of France'. In 1898, the École Française d'Extrême Orient started clearing the jungle, restoring the temples, mapping the complex and making an inventory of the site. Delaporte was later to write the two-volume *Les Monuments du Cambodge*, the most comprehensive Angkorian inventory of its time, and his earlier sketches, plans and reconstructions, published in *Voyage au Cambodge* in 1880 are without parallel.

The Churning of the Sea

The Hindu legend, the Churning of the Sea, relates how the gods and demons resolved matters in the turbulent days when the world was being created. The elixir of immortality was one of 13 precious things lost in the churning of the cosmic sea. It took 1000 years before the gods and demons, in a joint dredging operation – aided by Sesha, the sea snake, and Vishnu – recovered them all.

The design of the temples of Angkor was based on this ancient legend. The moat represents the ocean and the gods use the top of Mount Meru – represented by the tower – as their churning stick. The cosmic serpent offered himself as a rope to enable the gods and demons to twirl the stick.

Paul Mus, a French archaeologist, suggests that the bridge with the naga balustrades which went over the moat from the world of men to the royal city was an image of the rainbow. Throughout Southeast Asia and India, the rainbow is alluded to as a multi-coloured serpent rearing its head in the sky.

Angkor temples

The temples at Angkor were modelled on those of the kingdom of Chenla (a mountain kingdom centred on northern Cambodia and southern Laos), which in turn were modelled on Indian temples. They represent Mount Meru – the home of the gods of Indian cosmology. The central towers symbolize the peaks of Mount Meru, surrounded by a wall representing the earth and moats and basins representing the oceans. The devaraja, or god-king, was enshrined in the centre of the religious complex, which acted as the spiritual axis of the kingdom. The people believed their apotheosized king communicated directly with the gods.

The central tower sanctuaries housed the images of the Hindu gods to whom the temples were dedicated. Dead members of the royal and priestly families were accorded a status on a par with these gods. Libraries to store the sacred scriptures were also built within the ceremonial centre. The temples were mainly built to shelter the images of the gods – unlike Christian churches, Moslem mosques and some Buddhist pagodas, they were not intended to accommodate worshippers. Only priests, the servants of the god, were allowed into the interiors. The 'congregation' would mill around in open courtyards or wooden pavilions.

The first temples were of a very simple design, but with time they became more grandiose and doors and galleries were added. Most of Angkor's buildings are made from a soft sandstone which is easy to work. It was transported to the site from Phnom Kulen, about 30 km to the northeast. Laterite was used for foundations, core material, and enclosure walls, as it was widely available and could be easily cut into blocks. A common feature of Khmer temples was false doors and windows on the sides and backs of sanctuaries and other buildings. In most cases there was no need for well-lit rooms and corridors as hardly anyone ever went into them. That said, the galleries round the central towers in later temples, such as Angkor Wat, indicate that worshippers did use the temples for ceremonial circumambulation when they would contemplate the inspiring bas-reliefs from the important Hindu epic, *Ramayana* and *Mahabharata* (written between 400 BC and AD 200).

Despite the court's conversion to Mahayana Buddhism in the 12th century, the architectural ground-plans of temples did not alter much – even though they were based on Hindu cosmology. The idea of the god-king was simply grafted onto the new state religion and statues of the Buddha rather than the gods of the Hindu pantheon were used to represent the god-king. One particular image of the Buddha predominated at Angkor in which he wears an Angkor-style crown, with a conical top encrusted with jewellery.

Angkor Wat

The awe-inspiring sight of Angkor Wat, first thing in the morning, is something you're not likely to forget. Angkor literally means 'city' or 'capital' and it is the biggest religious monument ever built and certainly one of the most spectacular. The temple complex covers 81 ha. Its five towers are emblazoned on the Cambodian flag and the 12th-century masterpiece is considered by art historians to be the prime example of classical Khmer art and architecture. It took more than 30 years to build and is dedicated to the Hindu god Vishnu, personified in earthly form by its builder, the god-king Suryavarman II, and is aligned east to west.

Angkor Wat differs from other temples, primarily because it is facing westward, symbolically the direction of death, leading many to originally believe it was a tomb. However, as Vishnu is associated with the west, it is now generally accepted that it served both as a temple and a mausoleum for the king. Like other Khmer temple-mountains, Angkor Wat is an architectural allegory, depicting in stone the epic tales of Hindu mythology. The central sanctuary of the temple complex represents the sacred Mount Meru, the centre of the Hindu universe, on whose summit the gods reside. Angkor Wat's five towers symbolize Meru's five peaks; the enclosing wall represents the mountains at the edge of the world and the surrounding moat, the ocean beyond.

1 Angkor Wat

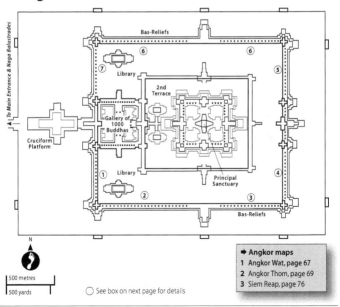

→ Angkor maps
1 Angkor Wat, page 67
2 Angkor Thom, page 69
3 Siem Reap, page 76

Anti-clockwise around Angkor Wat's bas-reliefs

1 Western gallery The southern half represents a scene from the Mahabharata of a battle between the Pandavas (with pointed head dresses, attacking from the right) and the Kauravas. The two armies come from the two ends of the panel and meet in the middle. The southwest corner has been badly damaged – some say by the Khmer Rouge – but shows scenes from Vishnu's life.

2 Southern gallery The western half depicts Suryavarman II (builder of Angkor Wat) leading a procession. He is riding a royal elephant, giving orders to his army before leading them into battle against the Cham. The rank of the army officers is indicated by the number of umbrellas. The undisciplined, outlandishly dressed figures are the Thais.

3 Southern gallery The eastern half was restored in 1946 and depicts the punishments and rewards one can expect in the after life. The damned are depicted in the bottom row, while the blessed, depicted in the upper two rows, are borne along in palanquins surrounded by large numbers of bare-breasted apsaras.

4 Eastern gallery The southern half is the best-known part of the bas-relief – the churning of the sea of milk by gods and demons to make ambrosia (the nectar of the gods which gives immortality). In the centre, Vishnu commands the operation. Below are sea animals and above, apsaras.

5 Eastern gallery The northern half is an unfinished representation of a war between the gods for the possession of the ambrosia. The gate in the centre was used by Khmer royalty and dignitaries for mounting and dismounting elephants.

6 Northern gallery Represents a war between gods and demons. Siva is shown in meditation with Ganesh, Brahma and Krishna. Most of the other scenes are from the Ramayana, notably the visit of Hanuman to Sita.

7 Western gallery The northern half has another scene from the Ramayana depicting a battle between Rama and Ravana who rides a chariot pulled by monsters and commands an army of giants.

The temple complex is enclosed by a square moat – more than 5 km in length and 190 m wide – and a high, galleried wall, which is covered in epic bas-reliefs and has four ceremonial tower gateways. The main gateway faces west and the temple is approached by a 475-m-long road, built along a causeway, which is lined with naga balustrades. At the far end of the causeway stands a **cruciform platform**, guarded by stone lions, from which the devaraja may have held audiences; his backdrop being the three-tiered central sanctuary. Commonly referred to as the Terrace of Honour, it is entered through the colonnaded processional gateway of the outer gallery. The transitional enclosure beyond it is again cruciform in shape. Its four quadrants formed galleries, once stocked full of statues of the Buddha. Only a handful of the original 1000-odd images remain.

The cluster of **central towers**, 12 m above the second terrace, is reached by 12 steep stairways, which represent the precipitous slopes of Mount Meru. Many historians believe that the upwards hike to this terrace was reserved for the high priests and king himself. Today, anyone is welcome but the difficult climb is best handled slowly by stepping sideways up the steep incline. The five lotus flower-shaped sandstone towers – the first appearance of these features in Khmer architecture – are believed to have once been covered in gold. The eight-storey towers are square, although they appear octagonal, and give the impression of a sprouting bud. The central tower is dominant, as is the Siva shrine and principal sanctuary, whose pinnacle rises more than 30 m above the third level and, 55m above ground level. This sanctuary would have contained an image of Siva in the likeness of King Suryavarman II, as it was his temple-mountain. But it is now a Buddhist shrine and contains statues of the Buddha.

More than 1000 sq m of bas-relief decorate the temple. Its greatest sculptural treasure is the 2-m-high **bas-reliefs**, around the walls of the outer gallery. It is the longest continuous bas-relief in the world. In some areas traces of the paint and gilt that once covered the carvings can still be seen. Most famous are the hundreds of figures of deities and apsaras in niches along the walls.

The royal city of Angkor Thom

Construction of Jayavarman VII's spacious walled capital, Angkor Thom (which means 'great city'), began at the end of the 12th century: he rebuilt the capital after it had been captured and destroyed by the Cham. Angkor Thom was colossal: the 100-m-wide moat surrounding the city, which was probably stocked with crocodiles as a protection against the enemy, extended more than 12 km. Inside the moat was an 8-m-high stone wall,

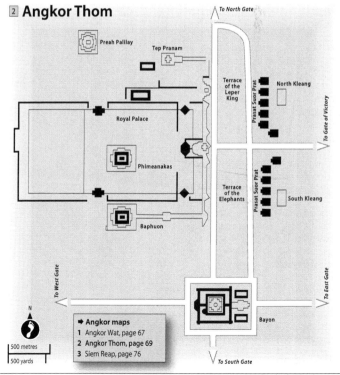

2 Angkor Thom

Preah Palilay

Tep Pranam

Terrace of the Leper King

North Kleang

Prasat Suor Prat

To Gate of Victory

To North Gate

Royal Palace

Phimeanakas

Terrace of the Elephants

Prasat Suor Prat

South Kleang

To West Gate

To East Gate

Baphuon

N

500 metres

500 yards

➡ Angkor maps
1 Angkor Wat, page 67
2 Angkor Thom, page 69
3 Siem Reap, page 76

Bayon

To South Gate

buttressed on the inner side by a high mound of earth along the top of which ran a terrace for troops to man the ramparts.

Four great gateways in the city wall face north, south, east and west and lead to the city's geometric centre, the Bayon. The fifth, Victory Gate, leads from the royal palace (within the Royal Enclosure) to the East Baray. The height of the gates was determined by the headroom needed to accommodate an elephant and howdah, complete with parasols. The flanks of each gateway are decorated by three-headed stone elephants, and each gateway tower has four giant faces, which keep an eye on all four cardinal points. Five causeways traverse the moat, each bordered by sculptured balustrades of nagas gripped, on one side, by 54 stern-looking giant gods and on the other by 54 fierce-faced demons. The balustrade depicts the Hindu legend of the churning of the sea (see box, page 66).

The **South Gate** provides the most common access route to Angkor Thom, predominantly because it sits on the path between the two great Angkor complexes. The gate is a wonderful introduction to Angkor Thom, with well-restored statues of asuras (demons) and gods lining the bridge. The figures on the left, exhibiting serene expression, are the gods, while those on the right, with grimaced, fierce-looking heads, are the asuras.

The **Bayon** was Jayavarman VII's own temple-mountain, built right in the middle of Angkor Thom; its large faces have now become synonymous with the Angkor complex. It is believed to have been built between the late 12th century to early 13th century, around 100 years after Angkor Wat. The Bayon is a three-tiered, pyramid-temple with a 45-m-high tower, topped by four gigantic carved heads. These faces are believed to be the images of Jayavarman VII as a Bodhisattra, and face the four compass points. They are crowned with lotus flowers, symbol of enlightenment, and are surrounded by 51 smaller towers each with heads facing north, south, east and west. There are more than 2000 large faces carved throughout the structure. The first two of the three levels feature galleries of bas-relief (which should be viewed clockwise); a circular central sanctuary dominates the third level. The **bas-reliefs** which decorate the walls of the Bayon are much less imposing than those at Angkor Wat. The sculpture is carved deeper but is more naive and less sophisticated than the bas-reliefs at Angkor Wat. The relief on the outside depicts historical events; those on the inside are drawn from the epic world of gods and legends, representing the creatures who were supposed to haunt the subterranean depths of Mount Meru. In fact the reliefs on the outer wall illustrating historical scenes and derring-do with marauding Cham were carved in the early 13th century during the reign of Jayavarman; those on the inside which illuminate the Hindu cosmology were carved after the king's death when his successors turned from Mahayana Buddhism back to Hinduism. Two recurring themes in the bas-reliefs are the powerful king and the Hindu epics. Jayavarman is depicted in the throes of battle with the Cham – who are recognizable thanks to their unusual and distinctive headdress, which looks like an inverted lotus flower. The other bas-reliefs give a good insight into Khmer life at the time – the warrior elephants, ox carts, fishing with nets, cockfights and skewered fish drying on racks. Other vignettes show musicians, jugglers, hunters, chess players, palm-readers and scenes of Angkor citizens enjoying drinking sessions. In the naval battle scenes, the water around the war-canoes is depicted by the presence of fish, crocodiles and floating corpses.

The **Royal Palace**, to the north of the Bayon, had already been laid out by Suryavarman I: the official palace was in the front with the domestic quarters behind, its gardens surrounded by a laterite wall and moat. Suryavarman I also beautified the royal city with ornamental pools. Jayavarman VII simply improved his designs. In front of the Royal Palace, at the centre of Angkor Thom, Suryavarman I laid out the first Grand Plaza with the **Terrace of the Elephants** (also called the Royal Terrace). The 300-m-long wall derives its name from the large, life-like carvings of elephants in a hunting scene, adorning its walls. The 2.5-m wall also features elephants flanking the southern stairway. It is believed it was the foundations of the royal reception hall. Royalty once sat in gold-topped pavilions at the centre of the pavilion, and here there are rows of garudas (bird-men), their wings lifted as if in flight. They were intended to give the impression that the god-king's palace was floating in the heavens, like the imagined flying celestial palaces of the gods. At the northeast corner of the 'central square' is the 12th-century **Terrace of the Leper King**, which may have been a cremation platform for the aristocracy of Angkor. The 7-m-high double terrace has bands of bas-reliefs, one on top of the other, with intricately sculptured scenes of royal pageantry and seated apsaras as well as nagas and garudas which frequented the slopes of Mount Meru. Above is a strange statue of an earlier date, which probably depicts the god of death, Yama, and once held a staff in its right hand. The statue's naked, lichen-covered body gives the terrace its name – the lichen gives the uncanny impression of leprosy. The **Phimeanakas** (meaning Celestial or Flying Palace in Sanskrit) inside the Royal Palace was started by Rajendravarman and used by all the later kings. Lions guard all four stairways to the central tower. It is now ruined but was originally covered in gold.

South of the Royal Palace is the **Baphuon**, built by Udayadityavarman II. The temple was approached by a 200-m-long sandstone causeway, raised on pillars, which was probably constructed after the temple was built. **Preah Palilay**, just outside the north wall of the Royal Palace, was also built by Jayavarman VII.

Around Angkor Thom

Phnom Bakheng

① *Either climb the steep hill (slippery when wet), ride an elephant to the top of the hill (US$15) or walk up the gentle zig-zag path the elephants take.*

Yasovarman's temple-mountain stands at the top of a natural hill, Phnom Bakheng, 60 m high, affording good views of the plains of Angkor. A pyramid-temple dedicated to Siva, Bakheng was the home of the royal linga and Yasovarman's mausoleum after his death. It is composed of five towers built on a sandstone platform. There are 108 smaller towers scattered around the terraces. The main tower has been partially demolished and the others have completely disappeared. It was entered via a steep flight of steps which were guarded by squatting lions. The steps have deteriorated with the towers. Foliate scroll relief carving covers much of the main shrine – the first time this style was used. This strategically placed hill served as a camp for various combatants, including the Vietnamese, and suffered accordingly.

Ta Pro

The temple of Ta Prohm is the perfect lost-in-the-jungle experience. Unlike most of the other monuments at Angkor, it has been only minimally cleared of its undergrowth, fig trees and creepers. It is widely regarded as one of Angkor's most enchanting temples.

Ta Prohm was consecrated in 1186 – five years after Jayavarman VII seized power. It was built to house the divine image of the Queen Mother. The outer enclosures of Ta Prohm are somewhat obscured by foliage but reach well beyond the temple's heart (1 km by 650 m). The temple proper consists of a number of concentric galleries, featuring corner towers and the standard gopuras. Other buildings and enclosures were built on a more ad hoc basis.

Within the complex walls lived 12,640 citizens. It contained 39 sanctuaries or prasats, 566 stone dwellings and 288 brick dwellings. Ta Prohm literally translates to the 'Royal Monastery' and that is what it functioned as, home to 18 abbots and 2740 monks. By the

12th century, temples were no longer exclusively places of worship – they also had to accommodate monks, so roofed halls were increasingly built within the complexes.

The trees burgeoning their way through the complex are predominantly the silk-cotton tree and the aptly named strangler fig. Naturally, the roots of the trees have descended towards the soil, prying their way through the temples foundations in the process. As the vegetation has matured, growing stronger, it has forced its way further into the temples structure, damaging the man-built base and causing untold destruction.

Banteay Kdei, Srah Srang, Prasat Kravan and Pre Rup

The massive complex of **Banteay Kdei**, otherwise known as 'the citadel of cells', is 3 km east of Angkor Thom. Some archaeologists think it may be dedicated to Jayavarman VII's religious teacher. The temple has remained in much the same state it was discovered in – a crowded collection of ruined laterite towers and connecting galleries lying on a flat plan, surrounded by a galleried enclosure. It is presumed that the temple was a Buddhist monastery and in recent years hundreds of buried Buddha statues were excavated from the site. Like Ta Prohm it contains a Hall of Dancers (east side), an open-roof building with four separate quarters. The second enclosure runs around the perimeters of the inner enclosure. The third inner enclosure contains a north and south library and central sanctuary. The central tower was never finished. The square pillars in the middle of the courtyard still cannot be explained by scholars. There are few inscriptions here to indicate either its name or purpose, but it is almost certainly a Buddhist temple built in the 12th century, about the same time as Ta Prohm. The Lake (baray) next to Banteay Kdei is called **Srah Srang** – 'Royal Bath' – and was used for ritual bathing. The steps down to the water face the rising sun and are flanked with lions and nagas. This sandstone landing stage dates from the reign of Jayavarman VII but the Lake itself is thought to date back two centuries earlier. A 10th-century inscription reads 'this water is stored for the use of all creatures except dyke breakers', eg elephants. The baray (700 m by 300 m), has been filled with turquoise-blue waters for more than 1300 years. With a good view of Pre Rup across the lake, some archaeologists believe that this spot affords the best vista in the whole Angkor complex.

Prasat Kravan, built in AD 921, means 'Cardamom Sanctuary' and is unusual in that it is built of brick. By that time brick had been replaced by laterite and sandstone. It consists of five brick towers arranged in a line. The Hindu temple, surrounded by a moat, consists of five elevated brick towers, positioned in a north-south direction. Two of the five decorated brick towers contain bas-reliefs (the north and central towers). The central tower is probably the most impressive and contains a linga on a pedestal. The sanctuary's three walls all contain pictures of Vishnu.

Northeast of Srah Srang is **Pre Rup**, the State Temple of King Rajendravarman's capital. Built in AD 961, the temple-mountain representing Mount Meru is larger, higher and artistically superior than its predecessor, the East Mebon, which it closely resembles. Keeping with tradition of state capitals, Pre Rup marked the centre of the city, much of which doesn't exist today. The pyramid-structure, which is constructed of laterite with brick prasats, sits at the apex of an artificial, purpose-built mountain. The central pyramid-level consists of a three-tiered, sandstone platform, with five central towers sitting above. Its modern name, 'turning the body', derives from local legend and is named after a cremation ritual in which the outline of a body was traced in the cinders one way and then the other. The upper levels of the pyramid offer a brilliant, panoramic view of the countryside.

Preah Khan

The 12th-century complex of Preah Khan, one of the largest complexes within the Angkor area, was Jayavarman VII's first capital before Angkor Thom was completed. Preah Khan means 'sacred sword' and is believed to have derived from a decisive battle against the Cham, which created a 'lake of blood', but was invariably won by Jayavarman VII. It is similar in ground-plan to Ta Prohm but attention was paid to the approaches: its east and west entrance avenues leading to ornamental causeways are lined with carved-stone boundary posts. Evidence suggests that it was more than a mere Buddhist monastery but most likely a Buddhist university. Nonetheless an abundance of Brahmanic iconography is still present on site. Around the rectangular complex is a large laterite wall, surrounded by large garudas wielding the naga (each more than 5 m in height), the theme continues across the length of the whole 3-km external enclosure, with the motif dotted every 50 m. Within these walls lies the surrounding moat.

Preah Neak Pean

To the east of Preah Khan is the Buddhist temple Preah Neak Pean built by Jayavarman VII. The temple of Neak Pean is also a fountain, built in the middle of a pool and representing the paradisiacal Himalayan mountain-lake, Anaavatapta, from Hindu mythology. It is a small sanctuary on an island in the baray of Preah Khan. Two nagas form the edge of the island, and their tails join at the back. The temple pools were an important part of the aesthetic experience of Preah Khan and Neak Pean – the ornate stone carving of both doubly visible by reflection.

Outlying temples

The Roluos Group

The Roluos Group receives few visitors but is worth visiting if time permits. Jayavarman II built several capitals including one at Roluos, at that time called Hariharalaya. This was the site of his last city and remained the capital during the reigns of his three successors. The three remaining Hindu sanctuaries at Roluos are **Preah Ko**, **Bakong** and **Lolei**. They were finished in AD 879, AD 881 and AD 893 respectively by Indravarman I and his son Yashovarman I and are the best-preserved of the early temples. All three temples are built of brick, with sandstone doorways and niches. Sculptured figures which appear in the Roluos group are the crouching lion, the reclining bull (Nandi – Siva's mount) and the naga (snake).

Preah Ko, meaning 'sacred ox', was named after the three statues of Nandi (the mount of the Hindu god, Siva) which stand in front of the temple. Orientated east-west, there is a cluster of six brick towers arranged in two rows on a low brick platform, the steps up to which are guarded by crouching lions while Nandi, looking back, blocks the way. The front row of towers was devoted to Indravarman's male ancestors and the second row to the female. Indravarman's temple-mountain, **Bakong**, is a royal five-stepped pyramid-temple with a sandstone central tower built on a series of successively receding terraces with surrounding brick towers. Indravarman himself was buried in the temple. Bakong is the largest and most impressive temple in the Roluos Group by a long way. A bridge flanked by a naga balustrade leads over a dry moat to the temple. The central tower was built to replace the original one when the monument was restored in the 12th century and is probably larger than the original. The Bakong denotes the true beginning of classical Khmer architecture and contained the god-king's Siva linga. **Lolei** was built by Yashovarman I in the middle of Indravarman's baray. The brick towers were dedicated to the king's ancestors, but they have disintegrated; of the four, two have partly collapsed.

Banteay Srei

Banteay Srei, 25 km from Ta Prohm along a decent road, was built by the Brahmin tutor to King Rajendravarman, Yajnavaraha, grandson of Harshavarman, and founded in AD 967. Banteay Srei translates to 'Citadel of Women', a title bestowed upon it in relatively recent years due to the intricate apsara carvings that adorn the interior. The temple is considered by many historians to be the highest achievement of art from the Angkor period. The explicit preservation of this temple reveals covered terraces, of which only the columns remain, which once lined both sides of the primary entrance. In keeping with tradition, a long causeway leads into the temple, across a moat, on the eastern side. The main walls, entry pavilions and libraries have been constructed from laterite and the carvings from pink sandstone. The layout was inspired by Prasat Thom at Koh Ker. Three beautifully carved tower-shrines stand side by side on a low terrace in the middle of a quadrangle, with a pair of libraries on either side enclosed by a wall. Two of the shrines, the southern one and the central one, were dedicated to Siva and the northern one to Vishnu; both had libraries close by, with carvings depicting appropriate legends. The whole temple is dedicated to Brahma. Having been built by a Brahmin priest, the temple was never intended for use by a king, which goes some way towards explaining its small size – you have to duck to get through the doorways to the sanctuary towers. Perhaps because of its modest scale Banteay Srei contains some of the finest examples of Khmer sculpture. Finely carved and rare pink sandstone replaces the plaster-coated carved-brick decoration, typical of earlier temples. All the buildings are covered in carvings: the jambs, the lintels, the balustered windows. Banteay Srei's ornamentation is exceptional – its roofs, pediments and lintels are magnificently carved with tongues of flame, serpents' tails, gods, demons and floral garlands.

Siem Reap → *For listings, see pages 75-83.*

The nearest town to Angkor, Siem Reap is a bustling tourism hub with a growing art and fashion crowd; however, it's still true to say that without the temples few people would ever find themselves here. Siem Reap is also an easy place to stay for volunteers looking to do a stint in saving the world, but perhaps too many nights spent in crowded bar street distracts from the task in hand. Visitors exhausted by the temple trail might care to while away a morning or afternoon in Siem Reap itself. The town has developed quite substantially in the past couple of years and, with the blossoming of hotels, restaurants and bars, it is now a pleasant place in its own right. Hotel building has pretty much kept pace with tourist arrivals so the town is a hive of activity.

The town is laid out formally and because there is ample land on which to build, it is pleasantly airy. Buildings are often set in large overgrown grounds resembling mini wildernesses. The current level of unprecedented growth and development is set to continue, so this may not be the case five years from now. The growth spurt has put a great strain on the city's natural resources.

The Old Market area is the most touristy part of the town. Staying around here is recommended for independent travellers and those staying more than two or three days. A sprinkling of guesthouses are here but a much greater selection is offered just across the river, in the Wat Bo area. This part of Siem Reap has recently become a popular place to stay with a range of accommodation available. It's not so crowded as the old market area and less traffic than airport road.

The **Angkor National Museum** ① *on the road to the temples, www.angkornationalmuseum. com, daily 0830-1800, US$12*, is a short walk from the town centre. Due to the high entry price this museum is usually empty and it does seem rather incongruous that the artefacts on display here are not actually still in-situ at the temples themselves. Having said that, it isn't a bad museum and you can gather a lot of useful information about the development of Angkor. There are also some intriguing background details such as the 102 hospitals built during the reign of Jayavarman VII and the 1960 boxes of haemorrhoid cream that were part of their annual provisions. There are also some displays on the clothes the average Angkorian wore but it's a shame there isn't more about the daily lives of these ancients.

Angkor listings

For hotel and restaurant price codes and other relevant information, see pages 8-9.

⊜ Where to stay

It is not uncommon for taxi, moto and tuk-tuk drivers to tell new arrivals that the guesthouse they were booked into is now 'closed' or full. They will try to take you to the place where they get the best commission. One way around this is to arrange for the guesthouse or hotel to pick you up from either the bus station or other arrival point – many offer this service for free or a small fee.

Siem Reap *p74, map p76*
$$$$ Angkor Village Resort, T063-963561, www.angkorvillage.com. Opened in 2004, the resort contains 40 rooms set in Balinese-style surroundings. Traditional massage services, 2 restaurants, theatre shows and lovely pool. Elephant, boat and helicopter rides can be arranged. Recommended.
$$$$ Heritage Suites, behind Wat Po Lanka, T063-969100, www.heritage.com.kh. Super luxurious and exclusive villas, rooms and suites in this stylish property secreted away behind a temple. Much is made with traditional materials and the top-end rooms come with private steam baths and gardens. A super-splurge but well worth it. Expect all the usual amneties for such a top-end establishment.
$$$$ Hotel de la Paix, corner of Achemean and Sivatha, T063-966000, www. hoteldelapaixangkor.com. This is probably Siem Reap's best-value luxury hotel. The rooms offer simple contemporary design with

giant bathtubs and plump bedding – all with a/c and cable TV. The pool is a maze of plinths and greenery and makes for a perfect spot to laze. Can feel a bit urban for Siem Reap but still a great hotel. Recommended.
$$$$ Le Meridien Angkor, main road towards temples, T063-963900, www. lemeridien.com/angkor. From the outside this 5-star hotel resembles a futuristic prison camp – severe, angled architecture with small, dark slits for windows. Walk into the lobby and it is immediately transformed into space and light. Rooms are nicely designed and sized and all come with a/c, en suite and cable TV. Other facilities include spa, restaurants and pool. The garden is a lovely spot to take breakfast. Recommended.
$$$$ La Residence D'Angkor Hotel, River Rd, T063-963390, www.residencedangkor. com. This is a hotel to aspire to. With its beautifully laid out rooms all lavishly furnished with marble and hardwoods, it is reassuringly expensive. Each room has a huge, free-form bath – which is the perfect end to a day touring the temples.
$$$$ Raffles Grand Hotel d'Angkor, 1 Charles de Gaulle Blvd, T063-963888, www. raffles.com. Certainly a magnificent period piece from the outside, Siem Reap's oldest (1930) hotel fails to generate ambience, the rooms are sterile and the design of the huge new wings is uninspired (unforgivable in Angkor). Coupled with this is a history of staff lock-outs and mass sackings that have caused the Raffles brand damage. However, it does have all the mod cons, including sauna, tennis, health and beauty spa, lap pool, gym, 8 restaurants and bars, nightly traditional

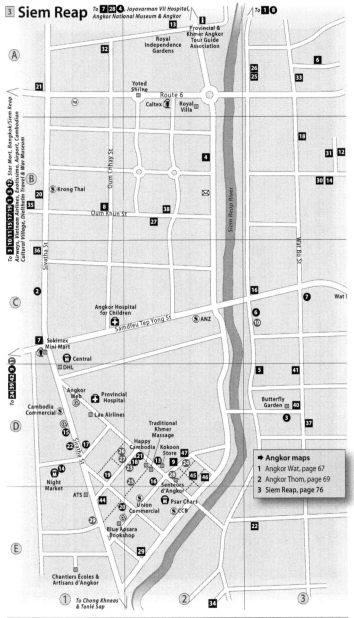

3 Siem Reap

To 7 28 4 Jayavarman VII Hospital, Angkor National Museum & Angkor

To 1 8

Provincial & Khmer Angkor Tout Guide Association

13

Royal Independence Gardens

32

26
25

6

33

Yoted Shrine

Route 6

Caltex

Royal Villa

21

To 3 10 11 15 17 19 1 3 12 Star Mart, Bangkok/Siem Reap Airways, Vietnam Airlines, Exotissimo, Airport, Cambodian Cultural Village, Dielthelm Travel & War Museum

Oum Chhay St

4

18

31 12

Krong Thai

20

30 14

35

8

38

27

Oum Khun St

Siem Reap River

Wat Bo St

36

2

16

Angkor Hospital for Children

ANZ

Samdeu Tep Yong St

7

Wat

6
10

Sokimex Mini Mart

7

Central

DHL

To 24 39 42 9

5

41

Angkor Web

Provincial Hospital

Lao Airlines

Traditional Khmer Massage

Butterfly Garden

40

3

37

Cambodia Commercial

15

22

Happy Cambodia

26
24

21

18

19

13

Kokoon Store

9

47

23

45 46

Senteurs d'Angkor

Sivatha St

Night Market

14

25

16

ATS

44

20

Union Commercial

Psar Chars

CCB

➡ Angkor maps
1 Angkor Wat, page 67
2 Angkor Thom, page 69
3 Siem Reap, page 76

29

Blue Apsara Bookshop

29

22

Chantiers Écoles & Artisans d'Angkor

1 To Chong Khneas & Tonlé Sap

2

3

34

N

100 metres
100 yards

Where to stay 🏨

Angkor Village Resort **1** A3
Angkor Palace Resort
  & Spa **17** A1
Apsara Angkor **3** C1
Bopha **5** D3
Bon Savy **19** A1
Borann **6** A3
Casa Angkor **8** B1
Earthwalkers **10** C1
Empress Angkor **11** B1
European Guesthouse
  12 B3
FCC **4** B2
Golden Banana B&B **34** E2
Green Garden Home
  Guesthouse **35** B1
Heritage Suites **23** A3
Home Sweet Home **14** B3
Hotel de la Paix **7** C1
Jasmine Lodge **15** B1
Jim's Place **9** D2
Kazna **24** C3
La Noria **26** A3
La Residence D'Angkor
  16 C3
Le Meridien Angkor **7** A2
Mahogany Guesthouse
  18 B3
Mekong Angkor Palace
  36 C1
Molly Malone's **44** E1
Neak Pean **20** B1
Neth Socheata **45** D2
Ombrelle & Kimono **37** D3
Passaggio **22** E2
Raffles Grand d'Angkor
  13 A2
Rosy Guesthouse **25** A3
Royal Bay Angkor Inn **38** B2
Sala Bai **39** C3
Shadow of Angkor I **46** D2
Shadow of Angkor II **40** D3
Shinta Mani **27** B2
Sofitel Royal Angkor **28** A2

Soria Moria **41** D3
Steung Siem Reap **47** D2
Sweet Dreams
  Guesthouse **31** B3
Ta Prohm **29** E2
Two Dragons Guesthouse
  30 B3
Victoria Angkor **32** A1
The Villa **42** C3
Villa Kiara **43** E3
Yaklom Angkor
  Lodge **33** A3

Restaurants 🍴

Abacus **1** A1
Barrio **2** C1
Blue Pumpkin **13** D2
Butterfly Gardens **3** D3
Chez Sophea **4** A2
Curry Walla **5** C1
Curry Walla II **14** D1
Dead Fish Tower **15** D1
Khmer Kitchen **16** D2
Le Malraux **17** D1
Le Tiore de Papier **18** D2
L'Oasi Italiana **8** A3
Moloppor **6** C3
Paul Dubrule **12** C1
Red Piano **19** D1
Singing Tree **20** E1
Soup Dragon **21** D1
Sugar Palm **9** C3
Tell **22** D1
Viroth's **7** C3
Pyongyang **3** B1

Bars & clubs 🍸

Angkor What? **23** D2
Fresh at Chili Si Dang **10** C3
Laundry **24** D2
Linga **25** D2
Miss Wong **26** D1
Temple Bar **27** D1
Warehouse **28** D2
X Rooftop Bar **29** E1
Zone One **11** C3

performances, landscaped gardens, 24-hr valet service and in-house movie channels. Considering its astronomical rates, guests have every right to feel disappointed.

$$$$ Shinta Mani, junction of Oum Khun and 14th St, T063-761998, www.shintamani. com. This 18-room boutique, luxury hotel is wonderful in every way: the design, the amenities, the food and the service. The hotel also offers a beautiful pool, library and has mountain bikes available. Provides vocational training to underprivileged youth.

$$$$ Sokha Angkor, Sivatha St, T063-969999, www.sokhahotels.com. One of the few Cambodian-owned 5-star hotels in the country, the rooms and services here are top notch, even if the decor is a little gaudy (if you can't afford to stay here, come and check out the incredibly over-the-top swimming pool, complete with faux temple structures and waterfalls). Also home to an excellent Japanese restaurant. Recommended.

$$$$ Victoria Angkor Hotel, Route 6, T063-760428, www.victoriahotels-asia.com. Perfection. A beautiful hotel, with that 1930s east-meets-west style that exemplifies the French tradition of *art de vivre*. The superb decor makes you feel like you are staying in another era. Each room is beautifully decorated with local fabrics and fantastic furniture. Swimming pool, open-air salas, jacuzzi and spa. It's the small touches and attention to detail that stands this hotel apart from the rest. Highly recommended.

$$$$-$$$ FCC Angkor, near the post office on Pokambor Av, T063-760280, www. fcccambodia.com. The sister property of the famous FCC Phnom Penh, this hotel is set in the grounds of a restored, modernist villa. Rooms offer contemporary luxury and plenty of space but be warned – there is a massive generator at one end of the complex running 24/7 so make sure you are housed well away from here. Also tends to trade more on its reputation so service, food, etc can be ropey.

$$$$-$$$$ Royal Bay Inn Angkor Resort, Oum Khon St, T063-760500, www. royalbayinnangkor.com. All rooms have balconies facing onto a huge swimming pool in this new resort, set in nice gardens. Expect the usual upmarket trimmings of a/c, multi-channel TV and good service.

$$$$-$$$ Steung Siem Reap Hotel, Street 9, T063-965167, www.steungsiem reaphotel.com. This new-build colonial-era-styled hotel is an excellent addition to the central market area of Siem Reap. The pleasant rooms come with cooling wooden floors and many overlook a verdant and very quiet pool. There are all the trimmings you'd expect in this price range, including gym, sauna, free Wi-Fi, free breakfast, a/c, huge bathtubs and good, friendly service.

$$$$-$$$ Villa Kiara, just outside eastern edge of town, Sala Kamroeuk village, T063-764156, www.villakiara.com. Set in a very peaceful, private garden compound a couple of kilometres east of town this 17-room/suite 'boutique' resort is unpretentious yet stylish. There's free breakfast, Wi-Fi, a restaurant and complimentary transfers to and from town. The pool is cute as well. All rooms are, of course, a/c with TV and en suite hot-water facilities. Recommended.

$$$ Ombrelle & Kimono, 557 Wat Bo Rd, T09-277 4313, www.ombrelleetkimono. com. There are only 5 rooms in this minute villa complete with pool and arty gardens. The rooms are a little pretentious but the welcome is friendly. All en suite, a/c and with private terrace.

$$$-$$ Casa Angkor, corner of Chhay St and Oum Khun St, T063-966234, www.casa angkorhotel.com. This is a good-looking, pleasant and well-managed 21-room hotel. 3 classes of room, all a decent size, well appointed and with cool wooden floors. Friendly reception and efficient staff. Restaurant, beer garden and reading room.

$$$-$$ La Noria, on road running on east side of the river, just past the 'stone' bridge, T063-964242, www.lanoriaangkor. com. Almost perfect riverside setting for this gorgeous small resort. Tranquil gardens, a small pool and a real away-from-it-all vibe seduces guests who stay in brightly

coloured a/c and en suite rooms each with their own balcony. No TV, very quiet and decent restaurant. Recommended.

$$$-$$ Molly Malone's, Old Market area, T063-963533, www.mollymalones cambodia.com. Fantastic rooms with 4-poster beds and good clean bathrooms. Irish pub downstairs. Lovely owners.

$$$-$$ Passaggio, near the Old Market, T063-760324, www.passaggio-hotel.com. 15 double and 2 family rooms, spacious, a/c, minibar and cable TV, internet, laundry service, bar and restaurant, outdoor terrace.

$$$-$$ Soria Moria, Wat Bo Rd, T063-964768, www.thesoriamoria.com. Excellent, well-run small hotel that has a roof-top bar and a decent restaurant. Rooms – all en suite, with contemporary Asian flourishes, a/c and colour TVs – are quiet; the upper ones have nice airy views over the town. The enlightened owners have now transferred half the ownership to their Khmer staff as part of an ongoing project to create sustainable, locally owned hotels in the area. Highly recommended.

$$ Borann, T063-964740, www.borann. com. This is an attractive hotel in a delightful garden with a pool. It is secluded and private. 5 small buildings each contain 4 comfortable rooms. Some have a/c, some fan only: price varies.

$$ Mekong Angkor Palace Hotel, 21 Sivatha Rd, T063-963636, www.mekong angkorpalaces.com. Excellent mid-range, great-value hotel in a good central location. All the spotless rooms are trimmed with a contemporary Khmer vibe, free Wi-Fi, a/c, hot-water bathrooms and TVs. Room rates also include breakfast and there's an excellent pool as well. Recommended.

$$ Shadow of Angkor II, Wat Bo Rd, T063-760363, www.shadowofangkor.com. Set on a quiet road this is the sister guesthouse of **Shadow of Angkor I** located on the market side of the river. This is another place offering well-located, good-value, well-run mid-range accommodation. As well as being clean and comfortable most rooms have balconies and all have a/c, free Wi-Fi, TV and hot water.

$$ The Villa, 153 Taphul St, T063-761036, www.thevillasiemreap.com. From the outside this place looks like a funky little guesthouse but some of the rooms are small and dark. All have a/c, TV and shower while the more expensive de luxe rooms are spacious and spotless.

$$-$ Bopha, on the east side of the river, T063-964928, www.bopha-angkor.com. Stunning hotel. Good rooms with all the amenities, decorated with local furniture and fabrics. Brilliant Thai-Khmer restaurant.

$$-$ Golden Banana Bed and Breakfast, Wat Damnak Area (past Martini Bar), T012-885366, www.goldenbanana.info. Good, clean rooms and decent restaurant.

$$-$ Home Sweet Home, T063-760279, www.homesweethomeangkor.com. Popular, and a favourite of the moto drivers (who get a kickback). Regardless, it's still got quite good, clean rooms, some with TV and a/c.

$$-$ Jasmine Lodge, Airport Rd near to town centre, T012-784980, www.jasmine lodge.com. One of the best budget deals in town, Jasmine is often fully booked, and with good reason. The super-friendly owner Kunn and his family go out of their way to make this a superlative place to stay; there's free internet and Wi-Fi, breakfast can be included in the rate on request, there are huge shared areas for sitting, a book exchange, tour bookings, bus tickets, etc. There is a huge spread of rooms from basic ones with a fan and shared facilities to sparkling new accommodation with a/c, TV and hot-water bathrooms. Highly recommended.

$$-$ Sala Bai, 155 Taphul Rd, T063-963329, www.salabai.com. Part of an NGO programme that trains disadvantaged young Cambodians to work in the hospitality industry. The rooms are decent enough, in a good location and the suite is an excellent deal. Cheaper rooms have fan, pricier ones a/c, all have private hot-water showers. Gets booked up so reserve in advance. See also Restaurants, page 80.

$$-$ Two Dragons Guesthouse, Wat Bo Village, T012-868551, twodragons-asia.com. Very pleasant, cleanrooms. Good little Thai restaurant. Gordon, the owner of this place, is one of the well-briefed guys in Siem Reap and runs www.talesofasia.com. He can organize a whole range of exciting tours around the area.

$ Bou Savy, just outside town off the main airport road, T063-964967, www.bousavy guesthouse.com. One of the best budget options in town this tiny and very friendly family-owned guesthouse is set in soothing gardens and offers a range of rooms with fan or a/c. They also offer breakfast, internet and have some nice public areas. Recommended.

$ Earthwalkers, just off the airport road, T012-967901, www.earthwalkers.no. Popular European-run budget guesthouse. Good gardens and pool table. Bit far out of town.

$ Mahogany Guesthouse, Wat Bo St, T063-963417/012-768944, proeun@big pond.com.kh. Fan and some a/c. An attractive and popular guesthouse, lovely wooden floor upstairs (try to avoid staying downstairs), coffee-making facilities and friendly guests.

$ Neth Socheata, 10 St Thnou, T063-963294, www.angkorguesthouseneth socheata.com. One of the Siem Reap's best deals, this small newly built budget guesthouse, tucked away down a quiet small alley opposite the market, has very nice, clean, pleasantly decorated rooms. All have en suite hot-water facilities and the price varies according to if you choose a/c or fan. The best rooms have small balconies while others are windowless. There's free Wi-Fi and a friendly welcome. Recommended.

Restaurants

Angkor *p60*
Near the moat there are a number of cheap food and drink stalls, bookshops and a posse of hawkers selling film, souvenirs, etc. Outside the entrance to Angkor Wat is a larger selection of cafés and restaurants

including the sister restaurant to **Blue Pumpkin**, serving good sandwiches and breakfasts, ideal for takeaway.

Siem Reap *p74, map p76*

$$$ Abacus, Oum Khun St, off Sivatha St, T012-644286. A little further out from the main Old Market area, this place is considered one of the best restaurants in town. Offering French and Cambodian, everything is fantastic here. The fish is superb, the steak is to die for. Recommended.

$$$ Barrio, Sivatha St, away from the central area. Fantastic French and Khmer food. A favourite of the expats. Recommended.

$$$ Chez Sophéa, outside Angkor Wat, T012-858003. A unique place in the evening serving Khmer and French cuisine. Romantic setting. It closes around 2100, but later if you want to stay for a digestif or two.

$$$ Le Malraux, Sivatha Bvld, T063-966041, www.le-malraux-siem-reap.com. Daily 0700-2400. Sophisticated French cuisine served in this excellent restaurant. Also do some Khmer and Asian dishes, great wine list and good cognacs. Patio or indoor seating.

$$$-$$ Sala Bai Restaurant School. See Where to stay, page 79. Open for breakfast and lunch only. Taking in students from impoverished backgrounds from the poorest areas of Cambodia, **Sala Bai** trains them in catering skills and places them in establishments around town. Service is not the best as students are quite shy practising their English, but a little bit of patience will help them through. Highly recommended.

$$$-$$ Soria Moria Fusion Kitchen, Wat Bo Road, T063-964768. Open 0700-2200. Serves a range of local, Scandinavian and Japanese specialities. Wed night is the popular US$1 night where all tapas dishes and drinks, including cocktails, cost US$1 each.

$$ The Blue Pumpkin, Old Market area, T063-963574. Western and Asian food and drinks. Sandwiches, ice cream, pitta, salads and pasta. Candidate for 'least likely eatery to find in Siem Reap' with its white minimalist decor reminiscent of the finest establishments in New York or London. Good breakfasts and cheap cocktails. Eat on the 2nd level. Branches at both the international and domestic terminals at the airport and across from Angkor. Recommended if you need a retreat for 30 mins.

$$ Bopha, on the east side of the river, slightly up from Passagio, T063-964928. Fantastic Thai-Khmer restaurant in lovely, tranquil garden setting. One of the absolute best in town. Highly recommended.

$$ Butterflies Gardens, just off Wat Bo Rd, T063-761211, www.butterfliesofangkor. com. Daily 0800-2200. Tropical butterflies flit around a koi-filled pond in this slightly odd eatery. The food is Khmer/Asian and is average but the setting is well worth a visit.

$$ Dead Fish Tower, Sivatha Blvd, T063-963060. Thai and Khmer restaurant in a fantastically eclectic modern Thai setting. Multiple platforms, quirky decorations, sculptures, apsara dance shows, small putting green and a crocodile farm all add to the atmosphere of this popular restaurant.

$$ Molly Malone's, T063-963533. Lovely Irish bar offering classic dishes like Irish lamb stew, shepherd's pie, roasts, and fish and chips.

$$ Red Piano, northwest of the Old Market, T063-963240. An institution in Siem Reap, based in a 100-year-old colonial building. Coffee, sandwiches, salad and pastas. Cocktail bar offering a range of tipples, including one dedicated to Angelina Jolie (who came here while working on Tomb Raider).

$$ Singing Tree, Wat Bo Rd, T09-263 5500, www.singingtreecafe.com. Tue-Sun 0800-2100. Brilliant diner-cum-community centre with tasty European and Khmer home cooking, with plenty of veggie options. Also host a DVD library and a fairtrade shop.

$$ Soup Dragon, T063-964933. Serves a variety of Khmer and Vietnamese dishes but its speciality is soups in earthenware pots cooked at the table. Breezy and clean, a light and colourful location. Upstairs bar, happy hour 1600-1930.

$$ The Sugar Palm, Taphul Road, T012-818143. Closed Sun. Sophisticated Khmer restaurant, with immaculate service with casual ambience.

$$ Tell, 374 Sivatha St, T063-963289. Swiss, German, Austrian restaurant and bar. Branch of the long-established Phnom Penh restaurant. Serves excellent fondue and raclette, imported beer and sausages. Reasonable prices and generous portions.

$$ Viroth's Restaurant, No 246 Wat Bo St, T016-951800. Upmarket place offering very good modern Khmer cuisine plus a few Western staples. Looks more expensive than it actually is, and is good value.

$ Khmer Kitchen, opposite Old Market and Alley West, T063-964154. Tasty cheap Khmer dishes service can be a little slow, but the food is worth waiting for. Sit on the alley side for good people-watching. Recommend their pumpkin pies (more of an omelette than a pie!).

$ Moloppor, east of the river, near Bopha Hotel. Good cheap Japanese and pizzas.

$ Paul Dubrule Hotel and Tourism School, airport road, about 3 km from town centre, T063-963672, www.ecolepauldubrule.org. Offers a pretty good set lunch. It can be hit and miss but the quality is often very high and they are always eager to keep their guests happy. Your money will also go to support an excellent vehicle for development: some of the school's graduates have gone on to be well-paid chefs at some of Asia's top hotels and restaurants.

🍸 Bars and clubs

Siem Reap *p74, map p76*

Angkor What?, Bar St, T012-490755. Friendly staff, popular with travellers and young expats.

Fresh at Chilli Si Dang, East River Rd, T017 875129. Open 0800-late. Laid back atmosphere, friendly service away from the tourist drag. Happy hour between 1700 and 2100.

Laundry, near the Old Market, turn right off 'Bar St', T012-246912. Open till late. Funky little bar.

Linga, Laneway behind 'Bar St', T012-246912. Gay-friendly bar offering a wide selection of cocktails. Great whiskey sours.

Miss Wong, The Lane (behind Pub St) T092-428332. Open 1700-0100. Cute little bar serving sharp cocktails in an Old Shanghai setting.

Temple Club, on 'Bar St', T015-999909. Popular drinking hole, dimly lit, good music. Not related to its seedier counterpart in Phnom Penh.

The Warehouse, opposite Old Market Area, T063-964600. Open 1000-0300. Popular bar, good service and Wi-Fi.

X Rooftop Bar, top of Sivataha St (you'll see the aluminous X from most high-rise buildings in town), T092-207842. Open 1600-sunrise. The latest closing bar in town. Happy hour 1600-1730.

Zone One, Taphul Village, T012-912347. Open 1800-late. The place to go to experience local nightlife.

☻ Entertainment

Siem Reap *p74, map p76*

Shadow puppetry

This is one of the finest performing arts of the region. The Bayon Restaurant, Wat Bo Rd, has regular shadow puppet shows in the evening. Local NGO, Krousar Thmey, often tour its shadow puppet show to Siem Reap. The show is performed by underprivileged children (who have also made the puppets) at La Noria Restaurant (Wed, 1930 but check as they can be irregular). Donations accepted.

A popular Sat evening attraction is the one-man concert put on by Dr Beat Richner (Beatocello), founder of the Jayavarman VII hospital for children. Run entirely on voluntary donations the 3 hospitals in the foundation need US$9 million per year in order to treat Cambodian children free of charge. He performs at the hospital, on the road to Angkor, at 1915, 1 hr, free admission but donations gratefully accepted. An interesting and worthwhile experience.

🛍 Shopping

Siem Reap p74, map p76

Outside Phnom Penh, Siem Reap is about the only place whose markets are worth browsing in for genuinely interesting souvenirs. **Old Market** (Psar Chars) is not a large market but stallholders and keepers of the surrounding shops have developed quite a good understanding of what tickles the appetite of foreigners: Buddhist statues and icons, reproductions of Angkor figures, silks, cottons, kramas, sarongs, silverware, leather puppets and rice paper rubbings of Angkor bas-reliefs are unusual mementos. In the night market area, off Sivatha St, you'll find bars, spas and cafés. The original night market, towards the back, has more original stalls, but is slightly more expensive.

Chantiers Écoles, down a short lane off Sivatha St, T063-963330. School for orphaned children that trains them in carving, sewing and weaving. Products are on sale under the name Les Artisans d'Angkor and raise 30% of the school's running costs.

Senteurs d'Angkor, opposite Old Market, T063-964801. Sells a good selection of handicrafts, carvings, silverware, silks, handmade paper, cards, scented oils, incense, pepper and spices.

🎯 What to do

Siem Reap p74, map p76

Helicopter and balloon rides For those wishing to see Angkor from a different perspective it is possible to charter a helicopter. In many ways, it is only from the air that you can really grasp the size and scale of Angkor and a short flight will certainly be a memorable experience. Try **Helicopters Cambodia**, T063-963316, www.helicopterscambodia.com, who offer flights from US$75 per person.

A cheaper (but not nearly as fun) alternative for a good aerial view is to organize a balloon ride above the temples. The tethered balloons float

200 m above Angkor Wat for about 10 mins, US$10 per trip. The balloon company is based about 1 km from the main gates from Angkor Wat, on the road from the airport to the temples.

Therapies Khmer, Thai, reflexology and Japanese massage are readily available. Many masseuses will come to your hotel.

Frangipani, Hup Guan St near Angkor Hospital for Children, T063-964391, www.frangipanisiemreap. Professional masseuse offers aromatherapy, reflexology and other treatments.

Mutita Spa, at Borei Angkor Resort and Spa on route 6, T63-964406. Offers unique J'Pong therapy, which is a traditional Cambodian heat and relaxation treatment using herbal steam.

Seeing Hands, Massage by sight-impaired individuals. US$3 per hr.

Tour operators

Asia Pacific Travel, 100 Route No 6, T063-760862, www.angkortravelcambodia.com. Tours of Angkor and the region.

Buffalo Tours, 556 Tep Vong St, Khum Svay Dangkom, T063-965670, www.buffalotours.com. Wide range of customised tours.

Exotissimo Travel, No 300, Highway 6, T063-964323, www.exotissimo.com. Tours of Angkor and sites beyond.

Hidden Cambodia Adventure Tours, T012-655201, www.hiddencambodia.com. Specializing in dirt-bike tours to remote areas and off-the-track temple locations. Recommended for the adventurous.

Journeys Within, on the outskirts of Siem Reap towards the temples, T063-966463, www.journeys-within.com. Customized tours, visiting temples and experiencing the everyday lives of Cambodians.

Terre Cambodge, on Huap Guan St near Angkor Hospital for Children, T092-476682, www.terrecambodge.com. Offers tours with a twist, including cruises on an old sampan boat. Not cheap but worth it for the experience.

Two Dragons Guesthouse, see page 79. Can also organize some off-the-beaten-

track tours. Owner Gordon Sharpless is a very knowledgeable and helpful fellow. **WHL Cambodia**, Wat Bo Road, T063-963854, www.angkorhotels.org. Local website booking hotels and tours with a responsible tourism approach.
World Express Travel, Street No11 (Old Market area), T063-963600. Can organize tours all over Cambodia. Also books local and international air/bus tickets. A good place to extend visas. Friendly service.

☉ Transport

Siem Reap *p74, map p76*
Air
Airline offices can be found in Siem Reap. Bangkok Airways, Airport Rd, www.bangkok air.com, 6 flights a day to **Bangkok**. Jetstar Asia, www.jetstarasia.com, flies to **Singapore** 3 times a week. Malaysian budget airlines **AirAsia**, T023-890035, www.airasia.com, to **Kuala Lumpur** daily. Helicopters Cambodia, 658 St Hup Quan, near Old Market, T063 963316, is a New Zealand company offering chartered flights around the temples. Lao Airlines, T/F063-963283, Mon-Fri 0800-1700 and Sat 0800-1200, flies to **Vientiane**, 3 times a week via **Pakse**. Malaysia Airlines, T063-964135, flies 3 times a week to **Kuala Lumpur**. Vietnam Airlines, Airport Rd, T063-964488, www. vietnamairlines.com, flies to **Ho Chi Minh City**. Silkair, T063-426 808, www.silkair.com, has daily flights to **Singapore**.

Bicycle
White Bicycles, www.thewhite bicycles. org, can be found at several hotels and guesthouses throughout Siem Reap. The White Bicycles scheme has been set up by expat Norwegian NGO workers as a way to provide not only a source of income and work for locals but also to develop a charitable fund that supports children and teenagers in Cambodia. The bikes cost US$2 a day to rent with US$1.50 going to the charitable fund and US$0.50 going to

sustain and repair the bikes by employing and training locals. **Khemara**, opposite the Old Market, T063-964512, rents bicycles for US$2 per day.

Bus
Neak Krorhorm Travel, GST, Mekong Express and Capitol go to and from Siem Reap. Most buses depart Phnom Penh bus station between 0630 and 0800 and the same from Siem Reap (departing near the Old Market). The best bus service is the Mekong Express, US$11, 5 hrs.

❶ Directory

Siem Reap *p74, map p76*
Banks ATMs can be found all over town. ANZ Royal, Old Market and Tep Vong St, T063-969700. Efficient friendly service. Cambodia Commercial Bank, 130 Sivatha St, currency and TC exchange, advance on Visa, MasterCard, JCB, AMEX. Mekong Bank, 43 Sivatha, Mon-Fri, Sat morning, US dollar TCs cashed, 2% commission, cash advance on Visa and JCB cards only. Union Commercial Bank, north of Old Market, Mon-Fri and Sat morning, cash advance on MasterCard and Visa (no commission), cash TCs. **Internet** Rates vary but should be around 3000 riel per hr. Most internet cafés now offer internet calls while most bars, restaurants, cafés and guesthouses have complimentary Wi-Fi for those using their services. **Medical services** Medical facilities are OK here and improving but by no means of an international standard. In most cases it's probably best to fly to Bangkok. Royal International Hospital, Airport Rd, T063-39911. Good standard and costs can be claimed back from most international insurance companies. Naga International Clinic, Highway 6 (airport road), T063-965988. International medical services. 24-hr emergency care. **Post office** Pokamber Av, on the west side of Siem Reap river, 0700-1700, but can take up to a month for mail to be delivered.

Background

Pre-history

Archaeological evidence suggests that the Mekong Delta and the lower reaches of the river – in modern-day Cambodia – have been inhabited since at least 4000 BC. But the wet and humid climate has destroyed most of the physical remains of the early civilizations. Excavated remains of a settlement at Samrong Sen on the Tonlé Sap show that houses were built from bamboo and wood and raised on stilts exactly as they are today. Where these people came from is uncertain but anthropologists have suggested that there were two waves of migration; one from the Malay peninsula and Indonesia and a second from Tibet and China.

Rise of the Lunar and Solar dynasties

For thousands of years Indochina was isolated from the rest of the world and was virtually unaffected by the rise and fall of the early Chinese dynasties. India and China 'discovered' Southeast Asia in the first millennium AD and trade networks were quickly established. The Indian influence was particularly strong in the Mekong basin. The Khmers adopted and adapted Indian script as well as their ideas about astrology, religion (Buddhism and Hinduism) and royalty (the cult of the semi-divine ruler). Today, several other aspects of Cambodian culture are recognizably Indian in origin, including classical literature and dance. Religious architecture also followed Indian models. These Indian cultural influences that took root in Indochina gave rise to a legend to which Cambodia traces its historical origins. An Indian Brahmin called Kaundinya, travelling in the Mekong Delta area, married Soma, daughter of the Naga (the serpent deity), or Lord of the Soil. Their union, which founded the 'Lunar Dynasty' of Funan (a pre-Angkorian Kingdom), symbolized the fertility of the kingdom and occupies a central place in Khmer cosmology. The Naga, Soma's father, helpfully drank the floodwaters of the Mekong, enabling people to cultivate the land.

Funan

The kingdom of Funan – the forerunner of Kambuja – was established on the Mekong by tribal people from South China in the middle of the third century AD and became the earliest Hindu state in Southeast Asia. Funan was known for its elaborate irrigation canals which controlled the Mekong floodwaters, irrigated the paddy fields and prevented the incursion of seawater. By the fifth century Funan had extended its influence over most of present-day Cambodia, as well as Indochina and parts of the Malay peninsula. Leadership was measured by success in battle and the ability to provide protection, and in recognition of this fact, rulers from the Funan period onward incorporated the suffix 'varman' (meaning protection) into their names. Records of a third-century Chinese embassy give an idea of what it was like: "There are walled villages, places and dwellings. The men ... go about naked and barefoot ... Taxes are paid in gold, silver and perfume. There are books and libraries and they can use the alphabet." Excavations conducted in the last 100 years or so suggest a seafaring people engaged in extensive trade with both India and China, and elsewhere.

The 'Solar Dynasty' of Chenla was a vassal kingdom of Funan, probably first based on the Mekong at the junction with the Mun tributary, but it rapidly grew in power, and was centred in the area of present-day southern Laos. It was the immediate predecessor of Kambuja and the great Khmer Empire. According to Khmer legend, the kingdom was the result of the marriage of Kambu, an ascetic, to a celestial nymph named Mera. The people of Chenla – the Kambuja, or the sons of Kambu – lent their name to the country. In AD 540 a Funan prince married a Chenla princess, uniting the Solar and Lunar dynasties. The prince sided with his wife and Funan was swallowed by Chenla. The first capital of this fusion was at **Sambor**. King Ishanavarman (AD 616-635) established a new capital at Sambor Prei Kuk, 30 km from modern Kompong Thom, in the centre of the country (the monuments of which are some of the best preserved of this period). His successor, Jayavarman I, moved the capital to the region of Angkor Borei near Takeo.

Quarrels in the ruling family led to the break-up of the state later in the seventh century: it was divided into 'Land Chenla', a farming culture located north of the Tonlé Sap (maybe centred around Champassak in Laos), and 'Water Chenla', a trading culture based along the Mekong. Towards the end of the eighth century Water Chenla became a vassal of Java's powerful Sailendra Dynasty and members of Chenla's ruling family were taken back to the Sailendra court. This period, from the fall of Funan until the eighth century, is known as the pre-Angkorian period and is a somewhat hazy time in the history of Cambodia. The Khmers remained firmly under Javanese suzerainty until Jayavarman II (AD 802-850) returned to the land of his ancestors around AD 800 to change the course of Cambodian history.

Angkor and the god-kings

Jayavarman II, the Khmer prince who had spent most of his life at the Sailendra court, claimed independence from Java and founded the Angkor Kingdom to the north of the Tonlé Sap in AD 802, at about the same time as Charlemagne became Holy Roman Emperor in Europe. They were men cast in the same mould, for both were empire builders. His far-reaching conquests at Wat Phou (Laos) and Sambhupura (Sambor) won him immediate political popularity on his return and he became king in AD 790. In AD 802 he declared himself a World Emperor and to consolidate and legitimize his position he arranged his coronation by a Brahmin priest, declaring himself the first Khmer devaraja, or god-king, a tradition continued today. From then on, the reigning monarch was identified with Siva, the king of the Hindu gods. In the centuries that followed, successive devaraja strove to outdo their predecessors by building bigger and finer temples to house the royal linga, a phallic symbol which is the symbol of Siva and the devaraja. The god-kings commanded the absolute allegiance of their subjects, giving them control of a vast pool of labour that was used to build an advanced and prosperous agricultural civilization. For many years historians and archaeologists maintained that the key to this agricultural wealth lay in a sophisticated hydraulic – that is irrigated – system of agriculture which allowed the Khmers to produce up to three harvests a year. However, this view of Angkorian agriculture has come under increasing scrutiny in recent years and now there are many who believe that flood-retreat – rather than irrigated – agriculture was the key. Jayavarman II installed himself in successive capitals north of the Tonlé Sap, secure from attack by the Sailendras, and he ruled until AD 850, when he died on the banks of the Great Lake at the original capital, Hariharalaya, in the Roluos area (Angkor).

Jayavarman III (AD 850-877) continued his father's traditions and ruled for the next 27 years. He expanded his father's empire at Hariharalaya and was the original founder of the laterite temple at Bakong. **Indravarman** (AD 877-889), his successor, was the first of the great temple-builders of Angkor and somewhat overshadowed the work of Jayavarman III. His means to succession are somewhat ambiguous but it is generally agreed that he overthrew Jayavarman III violently. Unlike his predecessor, Indravarman was not the son of a king but more than likely the nephew of Jayavarman's II Queen. He expanded and renovated the capital, building Preah Ko Temple and developing Bakong. Indravarman is considered one of the key players in Khmer history. Referred to as the "lion among kings" and "prince endowed with all the merits", his architectural projects established precedents that were emulated by those that followed him. After Indravarman's death his sons fought for the King's title. The victor, at the end of the ninth century was **Yasovarman I** (AD 889-900). The battle is believed to have destroyed the palace, thus spurring a move to Angkor. He called his new capital Yasodharapura and copied the water system his father had devised at Roluos on an even larger scale, using the waters of the Tonlé Sap. After Yasovarman's death in 900 his son **Harshavarman** (AD 900-923) took the throne, until he died 23 years later. Harshavarman was well regarded, one particular inscription saying that he "caused the joy of the universe". Upon his death, his brother **Ishanarvarman II**, assumed the regal status. In AD 928, **Jayavarman IV** set up a rival capital about 65 km from Angkor at Koh Ker and ruled for the next 20 years. After Jayavarman IV's death there was a period of upheaval as **Harsharvarman II** tried unsuccessfully to lead the empire. **Rajendravarman** (AD 944-968), Jayarvarman's nephew, managed to take control of the empire and moved the court back to Angkor, where the Khmer kings remained. He chose to build outside of the former capital Bakheng, opting instead for the region south of the East Baray. Many saw him as the saviour of Angkor with one inscription reading: "He restored the holy city of Yashodharapura, long deserted, and rendered it superb and charming." Rajendravarman orchestrated a campaign of solidarity – bringing together a number of provinces and claiming back territory, previously under Yasovarman I. From the restored capital he led a successful crusade against the Champa in what is now Vietnam. A devout Buddhist, he erected some of the first Buddhist temples in the precinct. Upon Rajendravarman's death, his son **Jayavarman V** (AD 968-1001), still only a child, took the royal reigns. Once again the administrative centre was moved, this time to the west, where Ta Keo was built. The capital was renamed Jayendranagari. Like his father, Jayavarman V was Buddhist but was extremely tolerant of other religions. At the start of his tenure he had a few clashes with local dissidents but things settled down and he enjoyed relative peace during his rule. The next king, **Udayadityavarman I**, lasted a few months before being ousted. For the next few years Suryavarman I and Jayaviravarman battled for the King's title.

The formidable warrior **King Suryavarman I** (1002-1049) won. He was a determined leader and made all of his officials swear a blood oath of allegiance. He undertook a series of military campaigns geared towards claiming Mon territory in central and southern Thailand and victoriously extended the Khmer empire into Lower Menam, as well as into Laos and established a Khmer capital in Louvo (modern day Lopburi in Thailand). Suryavarman holds the record for the greatest territorial expansion ever achieved in the Khmer Empire. The Royal Palace (Angkor Thom), the West Baray and the Phimeanakas pyramid temples were Suryavarman's main contributions to Angkor's architectural heritage. He continued the royal Hindu cult but also tolerated Mahayana Buddhism.

On Suryavarman's death, the Khmer Kingdom began to fragment. His three successors had short, troubled reigns and the Champa kingdom captured, sacked and razed the capital. When the king's son, **Udayadityavarman II** (1050-1066), assumed the throne, havoc ensued as citizens revolted against him and some of his royal appointments.

When Udayadityavarman II died, his younger brother, **Harsharvarman III** (1066-1080), last in the line of the dynasty, stepped in. During his reign, there were reports of discord and further defeat at the hands of the Cham.

In 1080 a new kingdom was founded by a northern provincial governor claiming aristocratic descent. He called himself **Jayavarman VI** (1080-1107) and is believed to have led a revolt against the former king. He never settled at Angkor, living instead in the northern part of the kingdom. He left monuments at Wat Phou in southern Laos and Phimai, in Thailand. There was an intermittent period where Jayavarman's IV brother, **Dharanindravarman** (1107-1112) took the throne but he was overthrown by his grandnephew **Suryavarman II** (1113-1150), who soon became the greatest leader the Angkor Empire had ever seen. He worked prolifically on a broad range of projects and achieved some of most impressive architectural feats and political manoeuvres seen within the Angkorian period. He resumed diplomatic relations with China, the Middle Kingdom, and was held in the greatest regard by the then Chinese Emperor. He expanded the Khmer Empire as far as Lopburi, Siam, Pagan in Myanmar, parts of Laos and into the Malay peninsula. He attacked the Champa state relentlessly, particularly Dai Vet in Northern Vietnam, eventually defeating them in 1144-1145, and capturing and sacking the royal capital, Vijaya. He left an incredible, monumental legacy behind, being responsible for the construction of Angkor Wat, an architectural masterpiece that represented the height of the Khmer's artistic genius, Phnom Rung temple (Khorat) and Banteay Samre. A network of roads was built to connect regional capitals.

However, his success was not without its costs – his widespread construction put serious pressure on the general running of the kingdom and major reservoirs silted up during this time; there was also an intensified discord in the provinces and his persistent battling fuelled an ongoing duel between the Cham and Khmers that was to continue (and eventually be avenged) long after his death.

Suryavarman II deposed the King of Champa in 1145 but the Cham regained their independence in 1149 and the following year, Suryavarman died after a disastrous attempt to conquer Annam (northern Vietnam). The throne was usurped by **Tribhuvanadityavarman** in 1165, who died in 1177, when the Cham seized their chance of revenge and sacked Angkor in a surprise naval attack. This was the Khmer's worst recorded defeat – the city was completely annihilated. The 50-year-old **Jayavarman VII** – a cousin of Suryavarman – turned out to be their saviour. He battled the Cham for the next four years, driving them out of the Kingdom. In 1181 he was declared king and seriously hit back, attacking the Chams and seizing their capital, Vijaya. He expanded the Khmer Kingdom further than ever before; its suzerainty stretched from the Malay peninsula in the south to the borders of Burma in the west and the Annamite chain to the northeast.

Jayavarman's VII's first task was to plan a strong, spacious new capital – Angkor Thom; but while that work was being undertaken he set up a smaller, temporary seat of government where he and his court could live in the meantime – Preah Khan meaning 'Fortunate City of Victory'. He also built 102 hospitals throughout his kingdom, as well as a network of roads, along which he constructed resthouses. But because they were built of wood, none of these secular structures survive; only the foundations of four larger ones have been unearthed at Angkor.

Angkor's decline

As was the case during Suryavarman II's reign, Jayavarman VII's extensive building campaign put a large amount of pressure on the kingdom's resources and rice was in short supply as labour was diverted into construction.

Jayavarman VII died in 1218 and the Kambujan Empire fell into progressive decline over the next two centuries. Territorially, it was eroded by the eastern migration of the Siamese.

The Khmers were unable to prevent this gradual incursion but the diversion of labour to the military rice farming helped seal the fate of Angkor. Another reason for the decline was the introduction of Theravada Buddhism in the 13th century, which undermined the prestige of the king and the priests. There is even a view that climatic change disrupted the agricultural system and led to Kambuja's demise. After Jayavarman VII, no king seems to have been able to unify the kingdom by force of arms or personality – internal dissent increased while the king's extravagance continued to place a crippling burden on state funds. With its temples decaying and its once-magnificent agricultural system in ruins, Angkor became virtually uninhabitable. In 1431 the royal capital was finally abandoned to the Siamese, who drove the Khmers out and made Cambodia a vassal of the Thai Sukhothai Kingdom.

Explaining Angkor's decline

Why the Angkorian Empire should have declined has always fascinated scholars in the West – in the same way that the decline and fall of the Roman Empire has done. Numerous explanations have been offered, and still the debate remains unresolved. As Anthony Barnett argued in a paper in the *New Left Review* in 1990, perhaps the question should be "why did Angkor last so long? Inauspiciously sited, it was nonetheless a tropical imperium of 500 years' duration."

There are essentially five lines of argument in the 'Why did Angkor fall?' debate. First, it has been argued that the building programmes became simply so arduous and demanding of ordinary people that they voted with their feet and moved out, depriving Angkor of the population necessary to support a great empire. Second, some scholars present an environmental argument: the great irrigation works silted up, undermining the empire's agricultural wealth. (This line of argument conflicts with recent work that maintains that Angkor's wealth was never based on hydraulic – or irrigated – agriculture.) Third, there are those who say that military defeat was the cause – but this only begs the question: why they were defeated in the first place? Fourth, historians with a rather wider view, have offered the opinion that the centres of economic activity in Southeast Asia moved from land-based to sea-based foci, and that Angkor was poorly located to adapt to this shift in patterns of trade, wealth and, hence, power. Lastly, some scholars argue that the religion that demanded such labour of Angkor's subjects became so corrupt that it ultimately corroded the empire from within.

After Angkor – running scared

The next 500 years or so, until the arrival of the French in 1863, was an undistinguished period in Cambodian history. In 1434 the royal Khmer court under Ponheayat moved to Phnom Penh, where a replica of the cosmic Mount Meru was built. There was a short-lived period of revival in the mid-15th century until the Siamese invaded and sacked the capital again in 1473. One of the sons of the captured King Suryavarman drummed up enough Khmer support to oust the invaders and there were no subsequent invasions during the 16th century. The capital was established at Lovek (between Phnom Penh and Tonlé Sap) and then moved back to the ruins at Angkor. But a Siamese invasion in 1593 sent the royal court fleeing to Laos; finally, in 1603, the Thais released a captured prince to rule over the Cambodian vassal state. There were at least 22 kings between 1603 and 1848.

Politically, the Cambodian court tried to steer a course between its powerful neighbours of Siam and Vietnam, seeking one's protection against the other. King **Chey**

Chetta II (1618-1628), for example, declared Cambodia's independence from Siam and in order to back up his actions he asked Vietnam for help. To cement the allegiance he was forced to marry a Vietnamese princess of the Nguyen Dynasty of Annam, and then obliged to pay tribute to Vietnam. His successors – hoping to rid themselves of Vietnamese domination – sought Siamese assistance and were then forced to pay for it by acknowledging Siam's suzerainty. Then in 1642, **King Chan** converted to Islam, and encouraged Malay and Javanese migrants to settle in Cambodia. Considering him guilty of apostasy, his cousins ousted him – with Vietnamese support. But 50 years later, the Cambodian **Ang Eng** was crowned in Bangkok. This see-saw pattern continued for years; only Siam's wars with Burma and Vietnam's internal disputes and long-running conflict with China prevented them from annexing the whole of Cambodia, although both took territorial advantage of the fragmented state.

By the early 1700s the kingdom was centred on Phnom Penh (there were periods when the king resided at Ondong). But when the Khmers lost their control over the Mekong Delta to the Vietnamese in the late 18th century, the capital's access to the sea was blocked. By 1750 the Khmer royal family had split into pro-Siamese and pro-Vietnamese factions. Between 1794-1811 and 1847-1863, Siamese influence was strongest; from 1835-1837 the Vietnamese dominated. In the 1840s, the Siamese and Vietnamese armies fought on Cambodian territory, devastating the country. This provoked French intervention – and cost Cambodia its independence, even if it had been nominal for several centuries anyway. On 17 April 1864 (the same day and month as the Khmer Rouge soldiers entered Phnom Penh in the 20th century) King Norodom agreed to French protection as he believed they would provide military assistance against the Siamese. The king was to be disappointed: France honoured Siam's claim to the western provinces of Battambang, Siem Reap and Sisophon, which Bangkok had captured in the late 1600s. And in 1884, King Norodom was persuaded by the French governor of the colony of Cochin China to sign another treaty that turned Cambodia into a French colony, along with Laos and Vietnam in the Union Indochinoise. The establishment of Cambodia as a French protectorate probably saved the country from being split up between Siam and Vietnam.

French colonial period

The French did little to develop Cambodia, preferring instead to let the territory pay for itself. They only invested income generated from tax revenue to build a communications network and from a Cambodian perspective, the only benefit of colonial rule was that the French forestalled the total disintegration of the country, which would otherwise have been divided up between its warring neighbours. French cartographers also mapped Cambodia's borders for the first time and in so doing forced the Thais to surrender the northwestern provinces of Battambang and Siem Reap.

For nearly a century the French alternately supported two branches of the royal family, the Norodoms and the Sisowaths, crowning the 18-year-old schoolboy **Prince Norodom Sihanouk** in 1941. The previous year, the Nazis had invaded and occupied France and French territories in Indochina were in turn occupied by the Japanese – although Cambodia was still formally governed and administered by the French. It was at this stage that a group of pro-independence Cambodians realized just how weak the French control of their country actually was. In 1942 two monks were arrested and accused of preaching anti-French sermons; within two days this sparked demonstrations by more than 1000 monks in Phnom Penh, marking the beginning of **Cambodian nationalism**. In March 1945 Japanese forces ousted the colonial administration and persuaded King Norodom

Sihanouk to proclaim independence. Following the Japanese surrender in August 1945, the French came back in force; Sihanouk tried to negotiate independence from France and they responded by abolishing the absolute monarchy in 1946 – although the king remained titular head of state. A new constitution was introduced allowing political activity and a National Assembly elected.

Independence and neutrality

By the early 1950s the French army had suffered several defeats in the war in Indochina. Sihanouk dissolved the National Assembly in mid-1952, which he was entitled to do under the constitution, and personally took charge of steering Cambodia towards independence from France. To publicize the cause, he travelled to Thailand, Japan and the United States, and said he would not return from self-imposed exile until his country was free. His audacity embarrassed the French into granting Cambodia independence on 9 November 1953 – and Sihanouk returned, triumphant.

The people of Cambodia did not want to return to absolute monarchy, and following his abdication in 1955, Sihanouk became a popular political leader. But political analysts believe that despite the apparent popularity of the former king's administration, different factions began to develop at this time, a process that was the root of the conflict in the years to come. During the 1960s, for example, there was a growing rift between the Khmer majority and other ethnic groups. Even in the countryside, differences became marked between the rice-growing lands and the more remote mountain areas where people practised shifting cultivation, supplementing their diet with lizards, snakes, roots and insects. As these problems intensified in the late 1960s and the economic situation deteriorated, the popular support base for the Khmer Rouge was put into place. With unchecked population growth, land ownership patterns became skewed, landlessness grew more widespread and food prices escalated.

Sihanouk managed to keep Cambodia out of the war that enveloped Laos and Vietnam during the late 1950s and 1960s by following a neutral policy – which helped attract millions of dollars of aid to Cambodia from both the West and the Eastern Bloc. But when a civil war broke out in South Vietnam in the early 1960s, Cambodia's survival – and Sihanouk's own survival – depended on its outcome. Sihanouk believed the rebels, the National Liberation Front (NLF) would win; and he openly courted and backed the NLF. It was an alliance which cost him dear. In 1965-1966 the tide began to turn in South Vietnam, due to US military and economic intervention. This forced NLF troops to take refuge inside Cambodia. When a peasant uprising in northwestern provinces in 1967 showed Sihanouk that he was sailing close to the wind his forces responded by suppressing the rebellion and massacring 10,000 peasants.

Slowly – and inevitably – he became the focus of resentment within Cambodia's political elite. He also incurred American wrath by allowing North Vietnamese forces to use Cambodian territory as an extension of the **Ho Chi Minh Trail**, ferrying arms and men into South Vietnam. This resulted in his former army Commander-in-Chief, **Marshal Lon Nol** masterminding Sihanouk's removal as Head of State while he was in Moscow in 1970. Lon Nol abolished the monarchy and proclaimed a republic. One of the most auspicious creatures in Khmer mythology is the white crocodile. It is said to appear 'above the surface' at important moments in history and is said to have been sighted near Phnom Penh just before Lon Nol took over.

Third Indochina War and the rise of the Khmer Rouge

On 30 April 1970, following the overthrow of Prince Norodom Sihanouk, US President Richard Nixon officially announced **Washington's military intervention in Cambodia** – although in reality it had been going on for some time. The invasion aimed to deny the Vietnamese Communists the use of Sihanoukville port through which 85% of their heavy arms were reaching South Vietnam. The US Air Force had been secretly bombing Cambodia using B-52s since March 1969. In 1973, facing defeat in Vietnam, the US Air Force B-52s began carpet bombing Communist-controlled areas to enable Lon Nol's inept regime to retain control of the besieged provincial cities.

Historian David P Chandler wrote: "When the campaign was stopped by the US Congress at the end of the year, the B-52s had dropped over half a million tons of bombs on a country with which the United States was not at war – more than twice the tonnage dropped on Japan during the Second World War.

The war in Cambodia was known as 'the sideshow' by journalists covering the war in Vietnam and by American policy-makers in London. Yet the intensity of US bombing in Cambodia was greater than it ever was in Vietnam; about 500,000 soldiers and civilians were killed over the four-year period. It also caused about two million refugees to flee from the countryside to the capital."

As Henry Kamm suggested, by the beginning of 1971 the people of Cambodia had to face the terrifying realisation that nowhere in the country was safe and all hope and confidence in Cambodia's future during the war was lost. A year after the coup d'etat the country was shattered: guerrilla forces had invaded Angkor, Lol Non had suffered a stroke and had relocated to Hawaii for months of treatment, Lol Non's irregularly paid soldiers were pillaging stores at gunpoint, and extreme corruption was endemic.

By the end of the war, the country had become totally dependent on US aid and much of the population survived on American rice rations. Confidence in the Lon Nol government collapsed as taxes rose and children were drafted into combat units. At the same time, the **Khmer Rouge** increased its military strength dramatically and began to make inroads into areas formerly controlled by government troops. Although officially the Khmer Rouge rebels represented the Beijing-based Royal Government of National Union of Cambodia (Grunc), which was headed by the exiled Prince Sihanouk, Grunc's de facto leaders were Pol Pot, Khieu Samphan (who, after Pol Pot's demise, became the public face of the Khmer Rouge), Ieng Sary (later foreign minister) and Son Sen (Chief of General Staff) – all Khmer Rouge men. By the time the American bombing stopped in 1973, the guerrillas dominated about 60% of Cambodian territory, while the government clung tenuously to towns and cities. Over the next two years the Khmer Rouge whittled away Phnom Penh's defence perimeter to the point that Lon Nol's government was sustained only by American airlifts into the capital.

Some commentators have suggested that the persistent heavy bombing of Cambodia, which forced the Communist guerrillas to live in terrible conditions, was partly responsible for the notorious savagery of the Khmer Rouge in later years. Not only were they brutalized by the conflict itself, but they became resentful of the fact that the city-dwellers had no inkling of how unpleasant their experiences really were. This, writes US political scientist Wayne Bert, "created the perception among the Khmer Rouge that the bulk of the population did not take part in the revolution, was therefore not enthusiastic about it and could not be trusted to support it. The final step in this logic was to punish or eliminate all in these categories who showed either real or imagined tendencies toward disloyalty". And that, as anyone who has watched *The Killing Fields* will know, is what happened.

'Pol Pot time': building year zero

On 1 April 1975 President Lon Nol fled Cambodia to escape the advancing Khmer Rouge. Just over two weeks later, on 17 April, the victorious Khmer Rouge entered Phnom Penh. The capital's population had been swollen by refugees from 600,000 to over two million. The ragged conquering troops were welcomed as heroes. None in the crowds that lined the streets appreciated the horrors that the victory would also bring. Cambodia was renamed Democratic Kampuchea (DK) and Pol Pot set to work establishing a radical Maoist-style agrarian society. These ideas had been first sketched out by his longstanding colleague Khieu Samphan, whose 1959 doctoral thesis – at the Sorbonne University in Paris – analyzed the effects of Cambodia's colonial and neo-colonial domination. In order to secure true economic and political independence he argued that it was necessary to isolate Cambodia completely and to go back to a self-sufficient agricultural economy.

Within days of the occupation, the revolutionaries had forcibly evacuated many of the inhabitants of Phnom Penh to the countryside, telling citizens that the Americans were about to bomb the capital. A second major displacement was carried out at the end of the year, when hundreds of thousands of people from the area southeast of Phnom Penh were forced to move to the northwest.

Prior to the Khmer Rouge coming to power, the Cambodian word for revolution (*bambahbambor*) had a conventional meaning, 'uprising'. Under Pol Pot's regime, the word *pativattana* was used instead; it meant 'return to the past'. The Khmer Rouge did this by obliterating everything that did not subscribe to their vision of the past glories of ancient Khmer culture. Pol Pot wanted to return the country to '**Year Zero**' – he wanted to begin again. One of the many revolutionary slogans was "we will burn the old grass and new will grow"; money, modern technology, medicine, education and newspapers were outlawed. Khieu Samphan, who became the Khmer Rouge Head of State, following Prince Sihanouk's resignation in 1976, said at the time: "No, we have no machines. We do everything by mainly relying on the strength of our people. We work completely self-sufficiently. This shows the overwhelming heroism of our people. This also shows the great force of our people. Though bare-handed, they can do everything".

The Khmer Rouge, or *Angkar Loeu* ('The Higher Organization') as they touted themselves, maintained a stranglehold on the country by dislocating families, disorientating people and sustaining a persistent fear through violence, torture and death. At the heart of their strategy was a plan to unfurl people's strongest bonds and loyalties: those that existed between family members. The term *kruosaa*, which traditionally means 'family' in Khmer, came to simply mean 'spouse' under the Khmer Rouge. In Angkar, family no longer existed. *Krusosaa niyum*, which loosely translated to 'familyism' (or pining for one's relatives) was a criminal offence punishable by death. Under heinous interrogation procedures people were intensively probed about their family members (sisters, brothers, grandparents and in-laws) and encouraged to inform on them. Those people who didn't turn over relatives considered adversaries (teachers, former soldiers, doctors, etc) faced odious consequences, with the fate of the whole family (immediate and extended) in danger.

Memoirs from survivors detailed in the book *Children of Cambodia's Killing Fields* repeatedly refer to the Khmer Rouge dictum "to keep you is no benefit to destroy you is no loss." People were treated as nothing more than machines. Food was scarce under Pol Pot's inefficient system of collective farming and administration was based on fear, torture and summary execution. A veil of secrecy shrouded Cambodia and, until a few desperate refugees began to trickle over the border into Thailand, the outside world was largely ignorant of what was going on. The refugees' stories of atrocities were, at first, disbelieved. Jewish refugees who escaped from Nazi occupied Poland in the 1940s had encountered a similarly disbelieving reception simply because (like the Cambodians) what they had to say was, to most people, unbelievable. Some left-wing academics initially viewed the revolution as an inspired and brave attempt to break the shackles of dependency and neo-colonial domination. Others, such as Noam Chomsky, dismissed the allegations as right wing press propaganda.

It was not until the Vietnamese 'liberation' of Phnom Penh in 1979 that the scale of the Khmer Rouge carnage emerged and the atrocities witnessed by the survivors became known. The stories turned the Khmer Rouge into international pariahs – but only until 1982 when, remarkably, their American and Chinese sympathizers secured them a voice at the United Nations. During the Khmer Rouge's 44-month reign of terror, it had hitherto been generally accepted that around a million people died. This is a horrendous figure when one considers that the population of the country in 1975 was around seven million. What is truly shocking is that the work undertaken by a team from Yale University indicates that this figure is far too low.

Although the Khmer Rouge era in Cambodia may have been a period of unprecedented economic, political and human turmoil, they still managed to keep meticulous records of what they were doing. In this regard the Khmer Rouge were rather like the Chinese during the Cultural Revolution, or the Nazis in Germany. Using Australian satellite data, the team was expecting to uncover around 200 mass graves; instead they found several thousand. The Khmer Rouge themselves have claimed that around 20,000 people died because of their 'mistakes'. The Vietnamese have traditionally put the figure at two to three million, although their estimates have generally been rejected as too high and politically motivated (being a means to justify their invasion of the country in 1978/1979 and subsequent occupation). The Documentation Center of Cambodia, involved in the heavy mapping project, said that 20,492 mass graves were uncovered containing the remains of 1,112,829 victims of execution. In addition, hundreds of thousands more died from famine and disease; frighteningly, the executions are believed to only account for about 30-40% of the total death toll.

How such a large slice of Cambodia's people died in so short a time (1975-1978) beggars belief. Some were shot, strangled or suffocated; many more starved; while others died from disease and overwork. The Khmer Rouge transformed Cambodia into what the British journalist, William Shawcross, described as: "a vast and sombre work camp where toil was unending, where respite and rewards were non-existent, where families were abolished and where murder was used as a tool of social discipline. The manner of execution was often brutal. Babies were torn apart limb from limb, pregnant women were disembowelled. Men and women were buried up to their necks in sand and left to die slowly. A common form of execution was by axe handles to the back of the neck. That saved ammunition".

The Khmer Rouge revolution was primarily a class-based one, fed by years of growing resentment against the privileged elites. The revolution pitted the least-literate, poorest rural peasants (referred to as the 'old' people) against the educated, skilled and foreign-influenced urban population (the 'new' people). The 'new' people provided an endless flow of numbers for the regime's death lists. Through a series of terrible purges, the members of the former governing and mercantile classes were liquidated or sent to work as forced labourers. But Peter Carey, Oxford historian and Chairman of the Cambodia Trust, argues that not all Pol Pot's victims were townspeople and merchants. "Under the terms of the 1948 Genocide Convention, the Khmer Rouge stands accused of genocide," he wrote in a letter to a British newspaper in 1990. "Of 64,000 Buddhist monks, 62,000 perished; of 250,000 Islamic Chams, 100,000; of 200,000 Vietnamese still left in 1975, 100,000; of 20,000 Thai, 12,000; of 1800 Lao, 1000. Of 2000 Kola, not a trace remained." American political scientist Wayne Bert noted that: "The methods and behaviour compare to that of the Nazis and Stalinists, but in the percentage of the population killed by a revolutionary movement, the Khmer Rouge holds an unchallenged record."

It is still unclear the degree to which these 'genocidal' actions were controlled by those at the centre. Many of the killings took place at the discretion of local leaders, but there were some notably cruel leaders in the upper echelons of the Khmer Rouge and none can have been ignorant of what was going on. Ta Mok, who administered the region southwest of Phnom Penh, oversaw many mass executions for example. There is also evidence that the central government was directly involved in the running of the Tuol Sleng detention centre in which at least 20,000 people died. It has now been turned into a memorial to Pol Pot's holocaust.

In addition to the legacy left by centres such as Tuol Sleng, there is the impact of the mass killings upon the Cambodian psyche. One of which is – to Western eyes – the startling openness with which Khmer people will, if asked, matter-of-factly relate their family history in detail: this usually involves telling how the Khmer Rouge era meant they lost one or several members of their family. Whereas death is talked about in hushed terms in Western society, Khmers have no such reservations, perhaps because it touched, and still touches, them all.

Vietnamese invasion

The first border clashes over offshore islands between Khmer Rouge forces and the Vietnamese army were reported just a month after the Khmer Rouge came to power. These erupted into a minor war in January 1977 when the Phnom Penh government accused Vietnam of seeking to incorporate Kampuchea into an Indochinese federation. Hanoi's determination to oust Pol Pot only really became apparent however, on Christmas Day 1978 when 120,000 Vietnamese troops invaded. By 7 January (the day of Phnom Penh's liberation) they had installed a puppet government which proclaimed the foundation of the People's Republic of Kampuchea (PRK): Heng Samrin, a former member of the Khmer Rouge, was appointed president. The Vietnamese compared their invasion to the liberation of Uganda from Idi Amin – but for the Western world it was unwelcome. The new government was accorded scant recognition abroad, while the toppled government of Democratic Kampuchea retained the country's seat at the United Nations.

The country's 'liberation' by Vietnam did not end the misery; in 1979 nearly half Cambodia's population was in transit, either searching for their former homes or fleeing across the Thai border into refugee camps. American political scientist Wayne Bert wrote: "The Vietnamese had long seen a special role for themselves in uniting and leading a greater Indochina Communist movement and the Cambodian Communists had seen with clarity that such a role for the Vietnamese could only be at the expense of their independence and prestige."

Under the Lon Nol and Khmer Rouge regimes, Vietnamese living in Cambodia were expelled or exterminated. Resentment had built up over the years in Hanoi – exacerbated by the apparent ingratitude of the Khmer Rouge for Vietnamese assistance in fighting Lon Nol's US-supported Khmer Republic in the early 1970s. As relations between the Khmer Rouge and the Vietnamese deteriorated, the Communist superpowers, China and the Soviet Union, polarized too – the former siding with the Khmer Rouge and the latter with

Hanoi. The Vietnamese invasion had the full backing of Moscow, while the Chinese and Americans began their support for the anti-Vietnamese rebels.

Following the Vietnamese invasion, three main anti-Hanoi factions were formed. In June 1982 they banded together in an unholy and unlikely alliance of convenience to fight the PRK and called themselves the Coalition Government of Democratic Kampuchea (CGDK), which was immediately recognized by the United Nations. The Communist **Khmer Rouge**, whose field forces recovered to at least 18,000 by the late 1980s were supplied with weapons by China and were concentrated in the Cardamom Mountains in the southwest and were also in control of some of the refugee camps along the Thai border. The National United Front for an Independent Neutral Peaceful and Co-operative Cambodia (Funcinpec) – known by most people as the **Armée Nationale Sihanoukiste** (ANS) was headed by Prince Sihanouk although he spent most of his time exiled in Beijing. The group had fewer than 15,000 well-equipped troops – most of whom took orders from Khmer Rouge commanders. The anti-Communist **Khmer People's National Liberation Front** (KPNLF), headed by Son Sann, a former prime minister under Sihanouk. Its 5000 troops were reportedly ill-disciplined in comparison with the Khmer Rouge and the ANS.

The three CGDK factions were ranged against the 70,000 troops loyal to the government of President Heng Samrin and Prime Minister Hun Sen (previously a Khmer Rouge cadre). They were backed by Vietnamese forces until September 1989. Within the forces of the Phnom Penh government there were reported to be problems of discipline and desertion. But the rebel guerrilla coalition was itself seriously weakened by rivalries and hatred between the different factions: in reality, the idea of a 'coalition' was fiction. Throughout most of the 1980s the war followed the progress of the seasons: during the dry season the PRK forces with their tanks and heavy arms took the offensive but during the wet season this heavy equipment was ineffective and the guerrilla resistance made advances.

Road towards peace

In the late 1980s the Association of Southeast Asian Nations (ASEAN) – for which the Cambodian conflict had almost become a raison d'être – began steps to bring the warring factions together over the negotiating table. ASEAN countries were united primarily in wanting the Vietnamese out of Cambodia. While publicly deploring the Khmer Rouge record, ASEAN tacitly supported the guerrillas. Thailand, an ASEAN member-state, which has had a centuries-long suspicion of the Vietnamese, co-operated closely with China to ensure that the Khmer Rouge guerrillas over the border were well-supplied with weapons.

After Mikhail Gorbachev had come to power in the Soviet Union, Moscow's support for the Vietnamese presence in Cambodia gradually evaporated. Gorbachev began leaning on Vietnam as early as 1987, to withdraw its troops. Despite saying their presence in Cambodia was 'irreversible', Vietnam completed its withdrawal in September 1989, ending nearly 11 years of Hanoi's direct military involvement. The withdrawal led to an immediate upsurge in political and military activity, as forces of the exiled CGDK put increased pressure on the now weakened Phnom Penh regime to begin power-sharing negotiations.

Modern Cambodia

In September 1989, under pressure at home and abroad, the Vietnamese withdrew from Cambodia. The immediate result of this withdrawal was an escalation of the civil war as the rebel factions tried to take advantage of the supposedly weakened Hun Sen regime in Phnom Penh. The government committed itself to liberalizing the economy and improving the infrastructure in order to undermine the political appeal of the rebels – particularly that of the Khmer Rouge. Peasant farmers were granted life tenancy to their land and collective farms were substituted with agricultural co-operatives. But because nepotism and bribery were rife in Phnom Penh, the popularity of the Hun Sen regime declined. The rebel position was further strengthened as the disparities between living standards in Phnom Penh and those in the rest of the country widened. In the capital, the government became alarmed; in a radio broadcast in 1991 it announced a crackdown on corruption claiming it was causing a "loss of confidence in our superb regime ... which is tantamount to paving the way for the return of the genocidal Pol Pot regime".

With the withdrawal of Vietnamese troops, the continuing civil war followed the familiar pattern of dry season government offensives, and consolidation of guerrilla positions during the monsoon rains. Much of the fighting focused on the potholed highways – particularly Highway 6, which connects the capital with Battambang – with the Khmer Rouge blowing up most of the bridges along the road. Their strategy involved cutting the roads in order to drain the government's limited resources. Other Khmer Rouge offensives were designed to serve their own economic ends – such as their capture of the gem-rich town of Pailin.

The Khmer Rouge ran extortion rackets throughout the country, even along the strategic Highway 4, which ferried military supplies, oil and consumer goods from the port of Kompong Som (Sihanoukville) to Phnom Penh. The State of Cambodia – or the government forces, known as SOC – was pressed to deploy troops to remote areas and allot scarce resources, settling refugees in more secure parts of the country. To add to their problems, Soviet and Eastern Bloc aid began to dry up.

Throughout 1991 the four warring factions were repeatedly brought to the negotiating table in an effort to hammer out a peace deal. Much of the argument centred on the word 'genocide'. The Prime Minister, Hun Sen, insisted that the wording of any agreement should explicitly condemn the former Khmer Rouge regime's 'genocidal acts'. But the Khmer Rouge refused to be party to any power-sharing deal which labelled them in such a way. Fighting intensified as hopes for a settlement increased – all sides wanted to consolidate their territory in advance of any agreement.

Rumours emerged that China was continuing to supply arms – including tanks, reportedly delivered through Thailand – to the Khmer Rouge. There were also accusations that the Phnom Penh government was using Vietnamese combat troops to stem Khmer Rouge advances – the first such reports since their official withdrawal in 1989. But finally, in June 1991, after several attempts, Sihanouk brokered a permanent ceasefire during a meeting of the Supreme National Council (SNC) in Pattaya, South Thailand. The SNC had been proposed by the United Nations Security Council in 1990 and formed in 1991, with an equal number of representatives from the Phnom Penh government and each of the resistance factions, with Sihanouk as its chairman. The following month he was elected chairman of the SNC, and resigned his presidency of the rebel coalition government in exile. Later in the year, the four factions agreed to reduce their armed guerrillas and militias by 70%. The remainder were to be placed under the supervision of the United Nations Transitional Authority in Cambodia (UNTAC), which supervised Cambodia's transition to multi-party democracy. Heng Samrin decided to drop his insistence that reference should be made to the former Khmer Rouge's 'genocidal regime'. It was also agreed that elections should be held in 1993 on the basis of proportional representation. Heng Samrin's Communist Party was promptly renamed the Cambodian People's Party, in an effort to persuade people that it sided with democracy and capitalism.

Paris Peace Accord

On 23 October 1991, the four warring Cambodian factions signed a peace agreement in Paris which officially ended 13 years of civil war and more than two decades of warfare. The accord was co-signed by 15 other members of the International Peace Conference on Cambodia. There was an air of unreality about the whole event, which brought bitter enemies face-to-face after months of protracted negotiations. There was, however, a notable lack of enthusiasm on the part of the four warring factions. Hun Sen said that the treaty was far from perfect because it failed to contain the word 'genocide' to remind Cambodians of the atrocities of the former Khmer Rouge regime and Western powers obviously agreed. But in the knowledge that it was a fragile agreement, everyone remained diplomatically quiet. US Secretary of State James Baker was quoted as saying "I don't think anyone can tell you there will for sure be lasting peace, but there is great hope."

Political analysts ascribed the successful conclusion to the months of negotiations to improved relations between China and Vietnam – there were reports that the two had held secret summits at which the Cambodia situation was discussed. China put pressure on Prince Norodom Sihanouk to take a leading role in the peace process, and Hanoi's new understanding with Beijing prompted Hun Sen's participation. The easing of tensions between China and Moscow – particularly following the Soviet Union's demise – also helped apply pressure on the different factions. Finally, the United States had shifted its position: in July 1990 it had announced that it would not support the presence of the Khmer Rouge at the UN and by September US officials were talking to Hun Sen.

On 14 November 1991, Prince Norodom Sihanouk returned to Phnom Penh to an ecstatic welcome, followed, a few days later, by Son Sen, a Khmer Rouge leader. On 27 November Khieu Samphan, who had represented the Khmer Rouge at all the peace negotiations, arrived on a flight from Bangkok. Within hours mayhem had broken out, and a lynch mob attacked him in his villa. Rumours circulated that Hun Sen had orchestrated the demonstration, and beating an undignified retreat down a ladder into a waiting armoured personnel carrier, the bloodied Khmer Rouge leader headed back to Pochentong Airport. The crowd had sent a clear signal that they, at least, were not happy to see him back. There were fears that this incident might derail the entire peace process – but in the event, the Khmer Rouge won a small public relations coup by playing the whole thing down. When the Supreme National Council (SNC) finally met in Phnom Penh at the end of December 1991, it was unanimously decided to rubberstamp the immediate deployment of UN troops to oversee the peace process in the run-up to a general election.

UN peace-keeping mission

Yasushi Akashi, a senior Japanese official in the United Nations, was assigned the daunting task of overseeing the biggest military and logistical operation in UN history. UNTAC comprised an international team of 22,000 peacekeepers – including 16,000 soldiers from 22 countries; 6000 officials; 3500 police and 1700 civilian employees and electoral volunteers. The first 'blue-beret' UN troops began arriving in November 1991, even before the SNC had agreed to the full complement of peacekeepers. The UN Advance Mission to Cambodia (UNAMIC) was followed four months later by the first of the main peacekeeping battalions. The odds were stacked against them. Shortly after his arrival, Akashi commented: "If one was a masochist one could not wish for more."

UNTAC's task

UNTAC's central mission was to supervise free elections in a country where most of the population had never voted and had little idea of how democracy was meant to work. The UN was also given the task of resettling 360,000 refugees from camps in Thailand and of demobilizing more than a quarter of a million soldiers and militiamen from the four main factions. In addition, it was to ensure that no further arms shipments reached these factions, whose remaining forces were to be confined to cantonments. In the run-up to the elections, UNTAC also took over the administration of the country, taking over the defence, foreign affairs, finance, public security and information portfolios as well as the task of trying to ensure respect for human rights.

Khmer Rouge pulls out

At the beginning of 1993 it became apparent that the Khmer Rouge had no intention of playing ball, despite its claim of a solid rural support base. The DK failed to register for the election before the expiry of the UN deadline and its forces stepped up attacks on UN personnel. In April 1993 Khieu Samphan and his entire entourage at the Khmer Rouge compound in Phnom Penh left the city. It was at this stage that UN officials finally began expressing their exasperation and anxiety over the Khmer Rouge's avowed intention to disrupt the polls. It was well known that the faction had procured fresh supplies of Chinese weapons through Thailand – although there is no evidence that these came from Beijing – as well as large arms caches all over the country.

By the time of the elections, the group was thought to be in control of between 10% and 15% of Cambodian territory. Khmer Rouge guerrillas launched attacks in April and May 1993. Having stoked racial antagonism, they started killing ethnic Vietnamese villagers and settlers, sending up to 20,000 of them fleeing into Vietnam. In one particularly vicious attack, 33 Vietnamese fishermen and their families were killed in a village on the Tonlé Sap. The Khmer Rouge also began ambushing and killing UN soldiers and electoral volunteers.

The UN remained determined that the elections should go ahead despite the Khmer Rouge threats and mounting political intimidation and violence between other factions, notably the Cambodian People's Party and Funcinpec. In the event, however, there were remarkably few violent incidents and the feared coordinated effort to disrupt the voting failed to materialize. Voters took no notice of Khmer Rouge calls to boycott the election and in fact, reports came in of large numbers of Khmer Rouge guerrillas and villagers from areas under their control, turning up at polling stations to cast their ballots.

UN-supervised elections

The days following the election saw a political farce – Cambodian style – which, as Nate Thayer wrote in the Far Eastern Economic Review "might have been comic if the implications were not so depressing for the country's future". In just a handful of days, the Phnom Penh-based correspondent went on, Cambodia "witnessed an abortive secession, a failed attempt to establish a provisional government, a royal family feud and the manoeuvres of a prince [Sihanouk] obsessed with avenging his removal from power in a military coup more than 20 years [previously]". The elections gave Funcinpec 45% of the vote, the CPP 38% and the BLDP, 3%. The CPP immediately claimed the results fraudulent, while Prince Norodom Chakrapong – one of Sihanouk's sons – announced the secession of the country's six eastern provinces. Fortunately, both attempts to undermine the election dissolved. The CPP agreed to join Funcinpec in a power-sharing agreement while, remarkably, the Khmer Rouge were able to present themselves as defenders of democracy in the face of the CPP's claims of vote-rigging. The new Cambodian constitution was ratified in September 1993, marking the end of UNTAC's involvement in the country. Under the new constitution, Cambodia was to be a pluralistic liberal-democratic country. Seventy-year-old Sihanouk was crowned King of Cambodia, reclaiming the throne he relinquished in 1955. His son Norodom Ranariddh was appointed First Prime Minister and Hun Sen, Second Prime Minister, a situation intended to promote national unity but which instead lead to internal bickering and dissent.

An uncivil society?

Almost from day one of Cambodia's rebirth as an independent state espousing the principles of democracy and the market, cracks began to appear in the rickety structure that underlay these grand ideals. Rampant corruption, infighting among the coalition partners, political intrigue, murder and intimidation all became features of the political landscape – and have remained so to this day. There are three bright spots in an otherwise pretty dismal political landscape. First of all, the Khmer Rouge – along with Pol Pot – is dead and buried. Second, while there have been coups, attempted coups, murder, torture and intimidation, the country does still have an operating political system with an opposition of sorts. And third, the trajectory of change in recent years has been upwards. But, as the following account shows, politics in Cambodia makes Italy seem a model of stability and common sense.

From the elections of 1993 through to 1998, relations between the two key members of the ruling coalition, the CPP and Funcinpec, went from bad to quite appalling. At the end of 1995 Prince Norodom Sirivudh was arrested for plotting to kill Hun Sen and the prime minister ordered troops and tanks on to the streets of Phnom Penh. For a while the capital had the air of a city under siege. Sirivudh, secretary-general of Funcinpec and King Norodom Sihanouk's half-brother, has been a vocal critic of corruption in the government, and a supporter of Sam Rainsy, the country's most outspoken opposition politician and the bane of Hun Sen's life. The National Assembly voted unanimously to suspend Sirivudh's immunity from prosecution. Few commentators really believed that Sirivudh had plotted to kill Hun Sen. In the end Hun Sen did not go through with a trial and Sirivudh went into self-imposed exile.

In 1996, relations between the CPP and Funcinpec reached another low. First Prime Minister Prince Norodom Ranariddh joined his two exiled brothers – princes Chakkrapong and Sirivudh – along with Sam Rainsy, in France. Hun Sen smelled a rat and when Ranariddh threatened in May to pull out of the coalition his worries seemed to be confirmed. Only pressure from the outside prevented a meltdown. Foreign donors said that continuing aid was contingent on political harmony, and ASEAN sent the Malaysian foreign minister to knock a few heads together. Some months later relations became chillier following the drive-by killing of Hun Sen's brother-in-law as he left a restaurant in Phnom Penh.

Things, it seemed, couldn't get any worse – but they did. In February 1997, fighting between forces loyal to Ranariddh and Hun Sen broke out in Battambang. March saw a grenade attack on a demonstration led by opposition leader Sam Rainsy outside the National Assembly leaving 16 dead and 150 injured – including Rainsy himself who suffered minor injuries. In April, Hun Sen mounted what became known as the 'soft coup'. This followed a complicated series of defections from Ranariddh's Funcinpec party to the CPP which, after much to-ing and fro-ing overturned Funcinpec's small majority in the National Assembly. In May, Hun Sen's motorcade was attacked and a month later, on 16 June, fighting broke out between Hun Sen and Ranariddh's bodyguards leaving three dead. It was this gradual decline in relations between the two leaders and their parties which laid the foundations for the coup of 1997.

In July 1997 the stage was set for Cambodia to join ASEAN. This would have marked Cambodia's international rehabilitation. Then, just a month before the historic day, on 5-6 June, Hun Sen mounted a coup and ousted Norodom Ranariddh and his party, Funcinpec, from government. It took two days for Hun Sen and his forces to gain full control of the capital. Ranariddh escaped to Thailand while the United Nations Centre for Human Rights reported that 41 senior military officers and Ranariddh loyalists were hunted down in the days following the coup, tortured and executed. In August the National Assembly voted to withdraw Ranariddh's immunity from prosecution. Five months later, in January 1998, United Nations High Commissioner for Human Rights Mary Robinson visited Cambodia and pressed for an investigation into the deaths – a request that Hun Sen rejected as unwarranted interference. ASEAN, long used to claiming that the Association has no role interfering in domestic affairs, found it had no choice but to defer Cambodia's accession. The coup was widely condemned and on 17 September the UN decided to keep Cambodia's seat vacant in the General Assembly.

Following the coup of 1997 there was some speculation that Hun Sen would simply ignore the need to hold elections scheduled for 26 July. In addition, opposition parties threatened to boycott the elections even if they did occur, claiming that Hun Sen and his henchmen were intent on intimidation. But despite sporadic violence in the weeks and months leading up to the elections, all parties ended up participating. It seems that intense international pressure got to Hun Sen who appreciated that without the goodwill of foreign aid donors the country would simply collapse. Of the 4.9 million votes cast – constituting an impressive 90% of the electorate – Hun Sen's Cambodian People's Party won the largest share at just over 41%.

Hun Sen offered to bring Funcinpec and the SRP into a coalition government, but his advances were rejected. Instead Rainsy and Ranariddh encouraged a series of demonstrations and vigils outside the National Assembly – which quickly became known as 'Democracy Square', à la Tiananmen Square. At the beginning of September 1998, following a grenade attack on Hun Sen's residence and two weeks of uncharacteristic restraint on the part of the Second Prime Minister, government forces began a crackdown on the demonstrators. A week later the three protagonists – Ranariddh, Sam Rainsy and Hun Sen – agreed to talks presided over by King Sihanouk in Siem Reap. These progressed astonishingly well considering the state of relations between the three men and two days later the 122-seat National Assembly opened at Angkor Wat on 24 September. In mid-November further talks between the CPP and Funcinpec led to the formation of a coalition government. Hun Sen became sole prime minister and Ranariddh chairman of the National Assembly. While the CPP and Funcinpec took control of 12 and 11 ministries respectively, with Defence and Interior shared, the CPP got the lion's share of the key portfolios. **Sam Rainsy** was left on the opposition benches. It was only after the political détente that followed the elections that Cambodia was given permission to occupy its UN seat in December 1998. At a summit meeting in Hanoi around the same time, ASEAN also announced that they had agreed on the admission of Cambodia to the grouping – which finally came through on 30 April 1999.

A return to some kind of normality

The year 1997 was the low point in Cambodia's stuttering return to a semblance of normality. The Asian economic crisis combined with the coup (see above) to rock the country back on its heels. On 3 February 2002 free, fair and only modestly violent local commune elections were held. The CPP won the vote by a landslide and although there is little doubt that Hun Sen's party used a bit of muscle here and there, foreign election observers decided that the result reflected the will of the 90% of the electorate who voted. The CPP, despite its iron grip on power, does recognize that democracy means it has to get out there and make a case. Around one third of the CPP's more unpopular commune chiefs were replaced prior to the election. Funcinpec did badly, unable to shake off the perception that it sold out its principles to join the coalition in 1998. The opposition Sam Rainsy Party did rather better, largely for the same reason: the electorate viewed it as standing up to the might of the CPP, highlighting corruption and abuses of power.

In July 2002 Hun Sen took on the rotating chairmanship of ASEAN and used a round of high-profile meetings to demonstrate to the region, and the wider world, just how far the country has come. Hun Sen, who hardly has an enviable record as a touchy-feely politician, used the chairmanship of ASEAN to polish his own as well as his country's credentials in the arena of international public opinion. But despite the PR some Cambodians are concerned that Hun Sen is becoming a little like Burma's Ne Win. Like Ne Win, Hun Sen seems to be obsessed with numbers. His lucky number is nine; in 2002 he brought the local elections forward by three weeks so that the digits in the date would add up to nine. In 2001 he closed down all Cambodia's karaoke bars. With over 20 years as prime minister there is no one to touch Hun Sen and he seems to revel in his strongman reputation. Judges bow to his superior knowledge of the judicial system; kings and princes acknowledged his unparalleled role in appointing the new king; many journalists are in thrall to his power. If even the most fundamental of rights are negotiable then it would seem that only Cambodia's dependence on foreign largesse constrains his wilder impulses.

Compared to its recent past, the last 10 years has been a period of relative stability for Cambodia. Political violence and infighting between parties continues to be a major problem – by international standards the elections were borderline unacceptable, although most of the major parties were reasonably satisfied with the results which saw Hun Sen's landslide victory. The 2003 election wasn't smooth-sailing either. Prior to the June 2003 election the alleged instructions given by representatives of the CPP to government controlled election monitoring organizations were: "If we win by the law, then we win. If we lose by the law, we still must win." Nonetheless a political deadlock arose, with the CPP winning a majority of votes but not the two-thirds required under the constitution to govern alone. The incumbent CPP-led administration assumed power and took on a caretaker role, pending the creation of a coalition that would satisfy the required number of National Assembly seats to form government. Without a functioning legislature, the course of vital legislation was stalled. After almost a year-long stalemate, the National Assembly approved a controversial addendum to the constitution, which allowed a new government to be formed by vote. The vote took place on July 15 2004, and the National Assembly approved a new coalition government, an amalgam of the CPP and FUNCINPEC, with Hun Sen at the helm as prime minister and Prince Norodom Ranariddh as president of the national assembly.

The government's democratic principles came under fire once again in February 2005, when opposition leader Sam Rainsy fled the country after losing his parliamentary immunity from prosecution. Rainsy is perceived as something of a threat due to his steadily gaining popularity with young urban dwellers, whose growing disenchantment with the current government he feeds off. On the one hand, his 'keep the bastards honest' style of politics has added a new dimension of accountability to Cambodian politics, but on the other, his nationalist, racist rantings, particularly his anti-Vietnamese sentiments, could be a very bad thing for the country. In May, 2005 Hun Sen said that Sam Rainsy would have to wait until the "next life" before he would guarantee his safety. However, having received a pardon in February 2006, he returned to the political fray soon after.

The lingering death of the Khmer Rouge
What many outsiders found hard to understand was how the Khmer Rouge enjoyed such popular support among Cambodians – even after the massacres and torture.

The Khmer Rouge was not, of course, just a political force. Its political influence was backed up and reinforced by military muscle. And it has been the defeat of the Khmer Rouge as an effective fighting force that seems to have delivered the fatal blow to its political ambitions.

In mid-1994 the National Assembly outlawed the Khmer Rouge, offering a six-month amnesty to rank-and-file guerrillas. By the time the six months was up in January 1995, 7000 Khmer Rouge had reportedly defected to the government, leaving at that time somewhere between 5000 and 6000 hardcore rebels still fighting. A split in this core group can be dated to 8 August 1996 when Khmer Rouge radio announced that former 'brother number two', Ieng Sary, had betrayed the revolution by embezzling money earned from mining and timber contracts, and branded him a traitor.

This was the first evidence available to Western commentators that a significant split in the Khmer Rouge had occurred. In retrospect, it seems that the split had been brewing for some years – ever since the UN-sponsored elections had revealed a division between 'conservatives' and 'moderates'. The latter, apparently, wished to co-operate with the UN, while the former group desired to boycott the elections. In 1996 the moderate faction, headed by Ieng Sary, finally broke away from the conservatives led by Pol Pot and hardman General Ta Mok. Hun Sen announced soon after the radio broadcast in August 1996 that two Khmer Rouge commanders, Ei Chhien and Sok Pheap had defected to the government. At the end of September Ieng Sary held a press conference to declare his defection. On 14 September King Norodom Sihanouk granted Ieng Sary a royal pardon.

The Cambodian government's conciliatory line towards Ieng Sary seemed perplexing given the man's past. Although he cast himself in the mould of 'misguided and ignorant revolutionary', there are few who doubt that he was fully cognisant of what the Khmer Rouge under Pol Pot were doing even if, as Michael Vickery argues, he was not Brother Number Two, just Brother Number Four or Five. Indeed he has admitted as much in the past. Not only is he, as a man, thoroughly unpleasant – or so those who know him have said – but he was also a key figure in the leadership and was sentenced to death in absentia by the Phnom Penh government. Stephen Heder of London's School of Oriental & African Studies was quoted as saying after the September press conference: "It's totally implausible that Ieng Sary was unaware that people were being murdered [by the Khmer Rouge]". The split in the Khmer Rouge and the defection of Ieng Sary deprived the Khmer Rouge of 3000-5000 men – halving its fighting force – and also denied the group important revenues from key gem mining areas around Pailin and many of the richest forest concessions.

The disintegration of the Khmer Rouge continued in 1997 after a complicated deal involving Pol Pot, Khieu Samphan, Son Sen and Ta Mok, as well as members of Funcinpec, collapsed. In early June Khieu Samphan, the nominal leader of the Khmer Rouge, was thought to be on the verge of brokering an agreement with Funcinpec that would give Pol Pot and two of his henchmen immunity from prosecution. This would then provide the means by which Khieu Samphan might enter mainstream Cambodian politics. It seems that Hun Sen, horrified at the idea of an alliance between Khieu Samphan and Funcinpec, mounted the coup of June 1997 to prevent the deal coming to fruition. Pol Pot was also, apparently, less than satisfied with the terms of the agreement and pulled out – killing Son Sen in the process. But before Pol Pot could flee, Ta Mok captured his erstwhile leader on June 19th at the Khmer Rouge stronghold of Anlong Veng.

A little more than a month later the 'Trial of the Century' began in this jungle hideout. It was a show trial – more like a Cultural Revolution lynching. A crowd of a few hundred people were on hand. Pol Pot offered the usual Khmer Rouge defence: the revolution made mistakes, but its leaders were inexperienced. And, in any case, they saved Cambodia from annexation by Vietnam. (There is an argument purveyed by some academics that the Khmer Rouge was essentially involved in a programme of ethnic cleansing aimed at ridding Cambodia of all Vietnamese people and influences.) Show trial or not, few people had any sympathy for Pol Pot as he was sentenced by the Khmer Rouge 'people's' court to life imprisonment for the murder of Son Sen. A Khmer Rouge radio station broadcast that with Pol Pot's arrest and sentencing, a 'dark cloud' had been lifted from the Cambodian people.

Confirmation of this bizarre turn of events emerged in mid-October when journalist Nate Thayer of the *Far Eastern Economic Review* became the first journalist to interview Pol Pot since 1979. He reported that the former Khmer Rouge leader was "very ill and perhaps close to death". Even more incredibly than Ieng Sary's defence, Pol Pot denied that the genocide had ever occurred and told Nate Thayer that his 'conscience was clear'.

In March 1998 reports filtered out of the jungle near the Thai border that the Khmer Rouge was finally disintegrating in mutinous conflict. The end game was at hand. The government's amnesty encouraged the great bulk of the Khmer Rouge's remaining fighters to lay down their arms and in December 1998 the last remnants of the rebel army surrendered to government forces, leaving just a handful of men under hardman 'The Butcher' Ta Mok still at large. But even Ta Mok's days of freedom were numbered. In March 1999 he was captured near the Thai border and taken back to Phnom Penh.

The death of Pol Pot
On 15 April 1998 unconfirmed reports stated that Pol Pot – a man who ranks with Hitler, Stalin and Mao in his ability to kill – had died in a remote jungle hideout in the north of Cambodia. Given that Pol Pot's death had been announced several times before, the natural inclination among journalists and commentators was to treat these reports with scepticism. But it was already known that Pol Pot was weak and frail and his death was confirmed when journalists were invited to view his body the following day. Pol Pot was reported to have died from a heart attack. He was 73.

A new era?
The question of what to do with Ieng Sary was the start of a long debate over how Cambodia – and the international community – should deal with former members of the Khmer Rouge. The pragmatic, realist line is that if lasting peace is to come to Cambodia, then it may be necessary to allow some people to get away with – well – murder. As one Western diplomat pondered: "Do you owe fealty to the dead for the living?" This would seem to be Hun Sen's preferred position.

By late 1998, with the apparent end of the Khmer Rouge as a fighting force, the government seemed happy to welcome back the rank and file into mainstream Cambodian life while putting on trial key characters in the Khmer Rouge like Ta Mok, Khieu Samphan

Buddhist Temple Wars and beyond

The stunning temple complex at Preah Vihear, pressed up tight on the remote regions of northern Cambodia, has long been a source of contention between Thailand and the Khmers. Since the colonial-era borders were established back in the early 20th century, Thailand has made repeated attempts to annex the area. However, in 1962, the argument was arbitrated by the International Court of Justice in The Hague which ruled that the temple fell within the boundaries of Cambodia. Unfortunately this was proved to be far from the last the international community saw of the dispute and over the years Preah Vihear has been at the centre of tensions between these neighbours.

In the 1990s Thailand suddenly closed access to the site, citing the illegal use of the border. In January 2003 there was further escalation of tensions after the misinterpretation of remarks allegedly made by a Thai actress insinuating that Thailand should regain control of the area. The Thai embassy in Phnom Penh was badly damaged in rioting along with many Thai-owned businesses. In May 2005 the two countries both deployed troops on the border surrounding Preah Vihear and while the troops, at that point, stood down, the situation remained testy.

Fast forward to 2008 and a longstanding application for Preah Vihear to be placed on the UNESCO World Heritage Site list came to fruition. Initially the Thai government supported the move, even though this meant accepting the contested areas were inside Cambodian territory. The thinking at the time was that the site could now benefit both nations.

With huge pressure coming to bear on the then Peoples' Power Party (PPP) goverment from the extreme fascistic nationalists of the Peoples' Alliance for Democracy (PAD), Thailand withdrew its support for UNESCO status and reneged on its promise to finally recognize Cambodia's claims. Nonetheless, UNESCO declared Preah Vihear a World Heritage Site in July 2008. Much sabre rattling ensued, with shots fired and military units mobilized. Thai nationalists were arrested by the Cambodians as they tried to plant a Thai flag in the Preah Vihear's grounds and bizarre black magic rituals were claimed to have been enacted by both sides. With the Thai foreign minister forced to resign and Thailand completely entrenched, a conflict seemed inevitable.

In October 2008 the fighting started in earnest with a mini-battle taking place that left several soldiers on both sides dead or injured. Thai nationals were advised to leave Cambodia by the Thai government and war seemed imminent. Fortunately, after intervention by the international community, both sides saw sense and pulled back from the brink.

In 2009 the situation continued to be tense, not least because the extremists of the PAD once again entered the fray holding a series of violent protests at the border. At one point they even threatened to attempt to storm the temple but the Cambodian government made it very clear they would shoot to kill if this took place. Skirmishes between both nations' armies then took place in April

and Nuon Chea. While the government was considering what to do, former leaders of the Khmer Rouge were busy trying to rehabilitate their muddied reputations. After years of living pretty comfortable lives around the country, particularly in and around Pailin, by late 2007 the old guard of the Khmer Rouge were finally being brought to book. This turn with several soldiers being killed. The PAD backed down and the situation was temporarily relieved.

In late 2009 Cambodian PM Hun Sen declared the Thai PM, Thaksin Shinawatra, who was deposed in a 2006 military coup, an economic adviser to Cambodia. For the ruling military-backed Thai Democrat Party government and their PAD allies, both of whom supported the military coup in 2006, this was a deliberate provocation by Hun Sen. Thailand recalled its ambassador, trade agreements were ripped up and the right-wing Thai press went into hysterics. For a short while it seemed like full-blown war might take place but, once again, both parties, amid calls for restraint from the international community, pulled back from the brink.

Tensions kept on ratcheting in 2010 and in early 2011 several Thai nationalists were arrested, including PAD members and a Democrat Party MP, after they attempted to walk into Cambodia, disregarding any border controls. The intention was to symbolically reassert Thai control over the disputed area and to seemingly provoking more fighting. The seven men were quickly arrested and thrown in a Phnom Penh prison. A few weeks later they achieved their desired effect and fighting broke out in earnest with several dead and an exchange of artillery and rocket fire that resulted in the Thais firing cluster munitions into Cambodia and drawing rebuke from the international community. With a Thai election drawing ever closer and the Democrat Party desperate to shore up

nationalist sentiment, war seemed, at some points, almost inevitable, but the Thai people, behaving far more rationally than their leaders in the military and government, had no enthusiasm for such a fight. After a few more skirmishes things calmed down and with the International Court of Justice ordering both countries to withdraw their troops and with a new Yingluck Shinawatra Pheu Thai Party government elected in July 2011 the possibility of more normal relations became a distinct possibility. By September 2011 MPs from Pheu Thai were in Cambodia playing in a football match with Hun Sen.

However, for those wishing to visit Preah Vihear we would advise closely following the situation at the time of travel. Parts of the Thai Army are desperate to destabilise the Yingluck government and a fight with Cambodia is very likely and one of the options they might consider in order to do so. Until this entire situation is at least partially resolved via binding, international legal norms we would suggest exercising great caution if you wish to travel there. Most foreign governments are still advising against travel to the temple. If you do visit we would recommend, at the very least, you take good advice from locals about the situation at time of travel and also use the services of a reputable tour operator or guide.

At the time of publication, the UK Foreign Office reported that the situation was improving and Cambodia withdrew nearly 500 troops from the area in July 2012.

of events was finally set in motion in March 2006 with the nomination of seven judges by the then Secretary General of the United Nations, Kofi Annan for the much anticipated Cambodia Tribunal. With Ta Mok dying in prison in early July 2006 the first charges were laid against the notorious head of the Tuol Sleng prison, Khang Khek Ieu, aka 'Comrade

Cambodia Tribunal

In 1997, with the country's interminable civil war set to end, the Cambodian government made an official approach to the UN to establish a court to prosecute senior members of the Khmer Rouge. The thinking at the time was that Cambodia lacked the institutions and know-how to handle such a big trial and that outside expertise would be needed.

At first, things for the prosecution looked promising, with an agreed handing over of Pol Pot (was holed up in northern Cambodia in Anlong Veng), set to take place in April 1998. But he never made it to court, mysteriously dying the night before his supposed arrest. Some say from a heart attack, others suspect that he took his own life.

In 1999, Kaing Guek Eav aka 'Comrade Duch', the commandant of the infamous Tuol Sleng prison camp in Phnom Penh, surrendered to the Cambodian authorities. In the same year, Ta Mok,

another blood-soaked Khmer Rouge leader, was also arrested (he died in custody seven years later in 2006). Initially, however, no power or legal authority existed to try them and it wasn't until 2001 that the Cambodian government agreed to pass a law setting up what came to be known as the 'Extraordinary Chambers in the Courts of Cambodia for the Prosecution of Crimes Committed during the Period of Democratic Kampuchea' or, for short, the Cambodia Tribunal.

Several more years passed, with the sometimes indifferent Cambodians stating that they had no money to finance the trials and the international community unwilling to fund a process in a country where corruption was so rampant. But despite this, in early 2006, buildings just outside Phnom Penh were requisitioned, the UN nominated its judges and by July of the same year a full

Duch'. Indicted on 31 July with crimes against humanity and after spending eight years behind bars, Duch is due to go on trial soon. Yet it was with the arrests in late 2007 of Ieng Sary, Nuon Chea and Khieu Samphan that the tribunal finally began to flex its muscles. Each of these arrests made international news and it seems, almost 30 years after the Vietnam invasion ended the abhorrent Khmer Rouge regime, that Cambodia may finally be coming to terms with its horrific past.

However, with only the few living key Khmer Rouge figures standing trial most of the minor – and probably equally murderous – cadre are still in circulation. It could be argued that the Tribunal is purely a diversion that allows this coterie of killers and Hun Sen's nefarious past to remain hidden from scrutiny.

What is obvious is that as the Tribunal progressed, many of the old divisions that have riven Cambodian society for generations where taking hold again. In late 2007 Cambodia was officially and internationally recognised as one of the most corrupt countries in history. Spend five minutes in Phnom Penh and this air of corruption is staring you in the face – Toyota Land Cruisers, giant, black Lexus SUVs and Humvees plough through the streets without regard for anyone or anything. When these vehicles do crush or kill other road users, the driver's well-armed body guards hop out, pistols waving, and soon dissuade any eager witnesses. This kind of event is commonplace and the poorer locals know this. Speak to a moto or tuk-tuk driver and you'll soon sense the resentment, "We hate the corrupt and we'd be happy to see them die", is a frequent comment reminiscent of Cambodia's darker times. The establishment of a rich new elite is not leading to the panel of 30 Cambodian and UN judges were fully sworn in. A list of five main suspects was drawn up in July 2007 and the first person formally charged was the already incarcerated Comrade Duch on 31 July 2007.

Then, in late 2007, after years of snail-like progress, and with the main protagonists approaching their twilight years, a flurry of dramatic arrests occurred. Former Khmer Rouge ideologue and Foreign Minister Ieng Sary and his wife, the Minister of Social Affairs, Ieng Thirith, former Chief of State and Pol Pot's number two, Khieu Samphan, were all taken into custody and charged with war crimes and crimes against humanity (their trials along with the former 'number two' in Pol Pot's regime, Nuon Chea, began in 2011).

The first trial of Extraordinary Chambers in the Courts of Cambodia for the Prosecution of Crimes Committed during the Period of Democratic Kampuchea began with Comrade Duch in February 2009. By the end of the same year his trial was over and in July 2010 Duch was found guilty of crimes against humanity, torture, and murder, receiving a 35-year prison sentence.

There's no doubt that Duch's public trial marked a turning point for Cambodia. For the first time the Khmer Rouge's crimes were aired in the cold, calculated and unambiguous efficiency of a courtroom. Victims confronted their tormentor with Duch expressing remorse and, more bizarrely, asking to be released by the court. With the first trial completed, and the trial of some of the Khmer Rouge's most senior figures now underway, a giant psychological hurdle was taken in its stride by the Cambodian people. Finally, after almost 40 years, it seems like justice will be delivered – this can only bode well for Cambodia's future.

trickle-down of wealth but the entrenchment of certain groups who have no regard at all for building a new society. Even the aid community is complicit in this – one senior worker made this damning off-the-record comment, "We view corruption as the only stabilizing factor in Cambodian society. It is awful but what else is there?"

The July 2008 general election changed little. Hun Sen was returned with an enlarged majority after a campaign that drew both praise and criticism from EU observers. On the upside the election was seen as being 'technically proficient' and possibly the best-run vote in Cambodia's history. Not that that's saying much; Hun Sen's ruling CPP was seen to have abused its position and not only dominated the media but also disenfranchised tens of thousands of opposition voters. Yet the same EU observers also felt the CPP would have won despite any machinations by Hun Sen and the vote was accepted in the international community. At the same time the election was taking place a row began to brew with Thailand over the contested Preah Vihear temple near the Thai/Cambodian border. In early July the Cambodian-led effort to turn the revered Preah Vihear into a UNESCO World Heritage Site was greeted by huge celebrations in Phnom Penh. For the Cambodians this meant that the long-contested temple was now firmly recognized as being in their territory. By early October 2008 a troop build-up escalated into an exchange of fire that led to a tense two-week stand-off and resulted in several deaths. Eventually, after pressure from the international community, both sides backed down but the dispute is still not settled and, at present, one of the region's most spectacular sites is off-limits.

It wasn't all bad news though as on 17 February 2009, 30 years after the fall of the Khmer Rouge regime, the first trial finally began against one of its former commanders began when Comrade Duch, the infamous commander of the Tuol Sleng death camp. As it progressed on through 2009, Duch's trial attracted a huge amount of international attention, not least for the plea the accused made in November 2009 to be released. While it must be said Duch has been one of the few senior Khmer Rouge leaders to have expressed any regret, this was still a staggering moment. By July 2010 a guilty verdict and a 35-year prison sentence had been handed down to Tuo Sleng's former custodian. By 2011 several of the other cases of remaining senior Khmer Rouge figures also began (see box, page 104) , and the process was still continuing at the time of publication.

The other main issue that has dominated Cambodia over the last period has been its relations with its neighbour, Thailand. Ostensibly focused on the disputed Preah Vihear temple (see box, page 104), this dispute has already reached the shooting stage on several occasions with soldiers on both sides being killed. There's also little doubt that the appointment of deposed Thai PM Thaksin – who is loathed by the controlling Thai elite and has been defined as a wanted 'criminal' by the Thai state – as an economic adviser by Hun Sen only exacerbated the situation. After Thaksin arrived in Cambodia in late 2009 the Thais withdrew their ambassador, threatened to tear up long-standing trade agreements and demanded that Cambodia, an ASEAN partner, arrest Thaksin and extradite him to Thailand to face a prison cell.

Hun Sen, with some justification, refused, citing that Thaksin's criminal conviction in Thailand was politicized and that Cambodia could choose who it wanted as an economic adviser. After the Thais threw a few more toys out of the pram, things calmed down enough for Hun Sen to visit Thailand for an ASEAN meeting and by mid-2010 it seemed as though the Thaksin element in Thai/Cambodia relations was no longer a defining factor.

Unfortunately, by 2011, the Preah Vihear issue, largely due to the antagonistic approach taken by extreme nationalists in Thailand, did reach a new nadir and for a while full-blown war looked like a possibility although the situation is now a lot calmer (see box, page 104). While Cambodia under Hun Sen's rule has made huge advances in recent years, and the Khmer Rouge trials clearly point to the nation finally coming to terms with itself, there is still a strong warrior streak running the Cambodian leader's character; maintaining peaceful relations with its turbulent and troublesome neighbour is key to Cambodia's ongoing development.

Contents

Footnotes

Index